Helpdesk Habits

Mark Copeman

Learn how to create and embed the right habits.
Become a helpdesk superhero
and make yourself indispensable.

"The subscription economy is drawing the relationship between your customer support team, reputation and brand ever closer.

As a result, your support and service operation holds one of the keys to your company's growth and profitability.

Mark's excellent, practical guide will provide a solid framework for anyone looking to build a career in support, or assist management in training and developing the skills, mentality and contribution of their team."

Lindsay Willott

CEO, Customer Thermometer

v1.3 | 2/21 Copyright © 2019 Mark Copeman

All rights reserved.

ISBN: 9781729416891

FOREWORD	8
INTRODUCTION	12
The ACETS pyramid	23
Introducing the pyramid	24
Attitude	25
Communications	25
Emotions	25
Tactics	25
Superhero habits	26
ATTITUDE	27
Introduction	28
Learn as much as you can	29
Remember Newton's 3rd Law	31
Have a wider purpose	34
The service recovery paradox	36
Just smile	39
Honesty is the best policy	42
Apologise. The right way	46
Be positive	50
Be human. Be you	52
COMMUNICATIONS	56
Introduction	57
Spelling and grammar matter	59
Use short sentences	62
Link externally	64

- Lay it out 66
- Tone of voice 69
- Phrase correctly 72
- Make it your job 75
- Hollow words and phrases 78
- I'd be happy to assist you with this today 82
- Give me a moment to look into that 84
- Using internal jargon 86
- As a gesture (of good faith) 88
- Is there anything else I can help you with? 90

EMOTIONS 93
- Introduction 94
- Understanding empathy 95
- Be forensic 97
- Create rapport 101
- State of mind 104
- Accept annoying bosses 106
- Difficult questions 108
- Delivering bad news 111
- Dealing with angry customers 115

TACTICS 119
- Introduction 120
- Understand urgency 121
- Keep your promises 125
- Unconscious selling 128

Encouraging complaints 132

Harvest testimonials 135

Check before sending 137

Let it sit 141

Always be documenting 143

Sharing is caring 147

Sign off sincerely 150

SUPERHERO HABITS 153

Introduction 154

Never assume 156

Never assume technical understanding 159

Anticipate like a Jedi 161

Solve the actual problem 164

Teach a man to fish 168

Managing 'quexpectations' 171

Refer, refer, refer 174

Get personal 176

Painting pictures 180

Roll your own 185

Register for a free trial at helpdeskhabits.com 187

ACKNOWLEDGMENTS

Writing this book has fulfilled a dream of mine.
I needed to get to the ripe old age of 47 to feel inspired enough to write it. That inspiration has come from many people. Many of whom are referenced within the habits.

My ex-business partner, Lindsay Willott, CEO of Customer Thermometer deserves the first mention. Without her tenacity and drive, my Customer Thermometer journey would have been much shorter and much less enjoyable. I learnt a huge amount from her during our time together. I must thank the amazing Customer Thermometer team too for their camaraderie and good nature during our 8 years together. I learnt so much from you all.

My family have been a huge inspiration to me over the years. My dad is mentioned several times in the habits. With his retirement looming, there's not much he doesn't know about dealing with customers and people. I think he's passed down some of that intuition.

Suzanne, my wife has taught me more than I'll ever know. Not necessarily about customer service, but about life and how to get the most from it. Kind, generous, supportive and caring, I lucked out when we met 25 years ago. Matthew and Lucy, our children, inspire me constantly and secretly seem quite proud of having a dad who's written an actual book.

I'm incredibly grateful to Jon Blakey and Tom Sopwith who were the first to read the book and provide a generous foreword, quotes and reviews. As two people I respect hugely in the IT support industry, I'm humbled by your kind words.

To the customers and colleagues, I've worked with over the last 25 years, thank you for helping me learn the art of rapport, empathy and customer service. I've got tougher over the years – but only because I know that's what you want.

Finally, I want to mention Daniel Priestley, author and founder of Dent Global. His books are inspirational. When I met him, he told me I needed to write a book. I now have.

FOREWORD

By Jon Blakey, CIO, The 20

As the great American writer Maya Angelou once said,

> *"I've learned that people will forget what you said, people will forget what you did, but people will never forget how you made them feel."*

From my personal experience working in customer service, as I put myself through college, to later on as an IT support technician, I found this to be 100% true. I used this as my motto and continued studying. Over the next decade, I have built a team of technicians and trained others on our team to hire for our industry-leading 24/7 support desk.

In my continued attempts to perfect hiring of the "ultimate technician", I came to find that this belief is not all that common, and the attitude and helpdesk habits that Mark talks about in this book should be the base foundation to becoming a support desk "superhero".

There are few books that address the personal attitude lens you must view customer service through, alongside the practical application of support desk habits that most companies struggle to put a finger on, which leave you feeling less than stellar about your client interactions.

I wholeheartedly believe that if you are in technical support, customer service, or have any part in hiring or training for these roles, this book is a must-read to rapidly increase competency and turn your company's hiring team into one that identifies and trains rock star agents. Putting these principles into place will be a key differentiator for your business.

In my role as CIO of The 20, an industry-leading IT service company, customer satisfaction is a key metric. I met Mark when we engaged his company, Customer Thermometer, to assist us with developing an improved software platform to better support our end clients. Mark's focus on the seemingly small things, even in his interaction with us, as a perspective client, was evident in our very first demo of their software. He created and prominently displayed a custom image combining The 20's logo with his own, helping us visualize our potential future partnership. This was probably a routine practice for him, but I still remember the impact it had on me.

As I got to know Mark, his expertise in customer service became overwhelmingly apparent. Questions about why his customer satisfaction gauge had four options instead of three (which I assumed was an arbitrary "because four is an even number and I like even numbers") was met with his citing of a psychological study that when presented with an odd number of options to rate, people overwhelmingly choose the middle option. As a service company, a neutral rating is essentially useless. By providing four options, the customer is forced to choose a positive or negative rating, resulting in more meaningful data.

With the help of Mark's vast knowledge of customer service, we've learned about the necessity of tracking customer feedback, coupled with it being quick and easy, and the importance of responding when we receive average or poor feedback. This has helped us attain a high nineties percentage average with good or great feedback for many years now using the same principles he has now outlined in this book.

So, soak up every bit of this information and remember, as every good superhero knows, "with great power, comes great responsibility."

Now, go out and be someone's helpdesk superhero!

Helpdesk Habits is available
as an online video program and certification.

Register for a free trial at **helpdeskhabits.com**

INTRODUCTION

Who will benefit from this book?

There are plenty of authors who concentrate on team work, helpdesk management, systems, bots, AI, automation and reducing headcount. That's not for me. I'm leaving them to do what they do best. I want to focus on us poor neglected humans.

"*Human* customer service" is a phrase I'm passionate about. Yes, the bots will come and go, but if I know human beings, we're going to want to interact with real people for decades to come. We as humans need to get better at having these interactions and stop hiding behind our bots and our knowledgebases. If we do, not only will your customers have a better day, you will too. I promise.

You will benefit from this book if you are involved in customer service in any capacity. Account managers, finance, marketers, HR (you have customers too, remember) will all find benefit. Developing new habits will mean you will think twice before sending that next email.

If you are a helpdesk agent or manager in the IT or software world, then this book is written specifically for you. Whether you are part of a service desk inside a large corporate organisation or a 5-person company helpdesk, I've seen with my own eyes the difference a focus on customer service and measuring the quality of that service can make. The topics in this book are practical and actionable and will help you make change as quickly as tomorrow.

The modern helpdesk spans many types of platform and so whether you spend your days on chat, on email threads, on the phone or forums, there's some habit forming gems in here for you.

If you spend the majority of your time speaking (as opposed to writing) to contacts, call centre agents will benefit from the habits and examples shown in the book too. The concepts span both the written word and speech.

It was time

Helpdesk Habits has been bubbling inside me for many years. I am *that person* who gives feedback, good or bad on a customer service experience. As I've got older, I've naturally got grumpier and those little customer service moments now really matter to me. If anything, they're amplified.

When an agent says or does (or doesn't) do something which just isn't right, it really does bother me. I'm assuming these types of behaviours therefore bother others. I can't be the only one, can I?

> **It costs five times as much to attract a new customer, than to keep an existing one.**

Sometimes I struggle to believe that agents don't realise the impact of what they're doing or saying.

Isn't it obvious when they're not getting it right?

Isn't it intuitive?

Having spoken to and worked with 100's of people around the world about customer service, satisfaction and loyalty over the last ten years, the simple answer to those questions are that no, good customer service, rapport and that sense of duty isn't necessarily intuitive.

The majority of people are not born with the customer service 'gene' and intuition to just do the right thing. To succeed, they need to be sat down and taught it.

As someone who has always had customer facing jobs, this has made me curious. Why don't people *naturally* do the right thing? Go the extra mile? Say and do the right things?

The conclusion I've come to, is that customer service is a skill and like any skill, it must be learnt. Unless you're taught to embrace this ethos and develop the right habits, many don't know why they should behave in certain ways, how to behave and importantly, understand why it matters *so much*.

Well, let me tell you, it really does matter.

Whether it's the (big German car manufacturer) service rep on the phone, blaming me for not booking a 'waiting car service appointment.' I didn't know this was a feature and wasn't even given the option for this feature ...

Whether it's the 1 hour 15 minute wait for that curry delivery, when you've been promised 20 mins ...

Whether it's the airline taking 90 mins to rebook a flight *they* cancelled and refused to call back (because the landline battery was about to give out) ...

It matters.

And yes, they've all happened to me over the last couple of months.

Can a customer ethos service be taught?

Maybe.

Can you be taught tactics, practice them regularly and aim to turn them into habits over time?

Definitely.

> *"Our character is basically a composite of our habits. Because they are consistent, often unconscious patterns, they constantly express our character."*
>
> **Stephen Covey**

Stephen knows a thing or two about habits, and writing for that matter, so I'll happily go along with his thinking on this. If our character is made up from our habits, and we get good at practicing customer service habits, then who says we can't eventually become natural at customer service?

This book aims to provide a series of "Aha" moments, and not in an Alan Partridge way (for UK readers) ... through a series of short essays, my aim is to show you the way, alongside practical suggestions of the words to be using, whether written or verbal.

Each topic can and should be used for conversation, in team meetings or in 1:1's. It's been proven that changing habits is easier when done as a group. Alcoholics Anonymous is an extreme, but excellent example of this happening every day.

> *There's something really powerful about groups and shared experiences. People might be sceptical about their ability to change if they're by themselves, but a group will convince them to suspend disbelief. A community creates belief.*
>
> Lee Ann Kskutas, Alcohol Research Group

A word on habits

I'd like to thank Charles Duhigg for his book, *The Power of Habit*. It's helped me to understand the power of developing and embedding habits and why they occur. It's a fascinating read.

There are three parts to forming or changing a habit:

The cue or trigger: something which you recognise as being the cause of a particular behaviour.

The routine: the behaviour following the trigger, which could be physical or emotional.

The reward: where the brain decides whether a habit is worth developing and filing under 'automatic mode'.

This is known as the habit loop.

Over time, these loops become more and more automatic, until a habit is born, and the anticipation and a sense of craving will eventually emerge.

Creating, changing or embedding a habit means firstly recognising the trigger which causes the routine or behaviour. If you can identify a trigger – the thing that you're doing to cause that bad behaviour or result, then you can work to *change* that behaviour, once triggered.

The reward at the end of each habit loop also needs to be worthwhile, for a new habit to embed.

At the end of each topic, you'll see a box summarising the old and new habit loops. Master the art of creating and changing habits and you'll be set for life.

What makes me qualified?

I've spent a lifetime in customer service. From the moment I left school and went to university, my fledgling DJ career saw me working society and hall balls at different venues all over Bristol here in the UK.

Skills such as empathy and rapport come in very handy at 2am when someone is screaming in your ear to play a particular record that you don't have. For readers under 40, there was a time when you didn't have every track ever produced in the palm of your hand. Ask your parents.

I had to learn quickly about how to deal with people – take their requests, apologise if I couldn't fulfil them, interact with the promoters and venue managers and deal with more than my fair share of problems. The wedding booking that ended up being a last-minute birthday gathering was an interesting evening. This job was my first experience of understanding how getting on with people can achieve great things.

I started my career in the UK's largest telco provider and was customer facing from day one, working with customers across all kinds of different projects. When you're working for such a large company, it may surprise you to know that things don't always go smoothly. I therefore realised early on, that customers are relying on you *as an individual* to be the conduit into the beast that is BT, (British Telecom), to get things done. Without tenacity and persistence and communication, your customer could easily be left hanging. Your involvement could often make a tangible difference to their day.

In 2000, I started the first of my two marketing and video production agencies. When you're running your own business (as I have done ever since), customer service underpins your whole day. You're not going to succeed if you don't get that part of your role under control. You deal with the good times, but you learn most in times of crisis and in small business, there's often crisis!

In 2010, I earnt the equivalent of my masters in customer service, as I co-founded Customer Thermometer, the still very awesome 1-click survey feedback tool. When you start a SaaS (software as a service) business, particularly back then, where there was very little written about the start-up world, you really don't know what you're getting in to.

When you're starting a business, which focuses and supports those in the customer service domain and you're looking to provide support via your *own* helpdesk (as I spent a lot of my time doing in the early days), then you must learn quickly.

Over the course of those 8 years, I presented the service to 100's of people... I answered tickets from 1,000+ people and helped to create a team, which to this day continues to support a growing customer base.

I learnt that customers were lazy, ignorant, wonderful, humorous, frustrating, rewarding and each one unique.

Customer service truly is the differentiator in this space. How fascinating it was to see our customers spreading the word about the awesome Ministry of Magic we set up, as we empowered our team, to always do the right thing.

So many of the lessons we learnt, are in this book. They are transferrable across all types of businesses but will resonate particularly in the IT and software helpdesk world.

A life changing experience

Before we dig in to the good stuff, I did want to tell one story, which will stay with me forever, for all kinds of reasons. Over time, it has helped to shape me and has made me really appreciate the value good customer service can bring.

It was a Friday afternoon in May 2012. (Why is it always a Friday?) I got a call from a customer of ours. They were one of the first adopters of the service and had put a huge amount of faith in our service to get results. They were a FTSE 100 organisation.

Unknown to us, they had used their account to do something we'd never seen before. They'd sent a survey to tens of thousands of people. It's not something we'd ever tested at the time as we were only a few months into our evolution. They had sent that survey to one of *their* biggest customers (also FTSE100). Senior execs from both sides were sat in the same room, eagerly staring at giant dashboards, waiting for results to come in, in real time.

The phone call was a bolt out of the blue. The customer told me that the CIO of the receiving organisation had received multiple copies of the survey and they were getting complaints of spam from across their business.

I wanted the ground to swallow me up.

I got on the phone to the team to dig into the issue and we quickly saw there had been an issue. The software hadn't been able to process the surveys fast enough and so had started sending duplicates and triplicates and so on.

Phone calls kept coming in from more and more irate execs. The fact they were in the same room made the situation worse. I literally felt sick.

Fortunately, we didn't have many customers at this point and so we shut the service down for the afternoon and went into fact finding and debugging mode. I could feel the weight of this company's legal team on our shoulders and all I wanted to do was to run away.

We worked tirelessly all weekend. We coded, we ran tests, thought through solutions and wrote a 20 page document for our customer, which identified exactly what happened, pinpointed exactly who got how many duplicates, described our remedial plan and I got ready to present it back to them on Monday afternoon.

By putting in that effort, by *not* putting our heads in the sand, by *not* giving up and facing up to the issue, we were subsequently told it was the best remedial report they had ever seen (clearly, they had seen a few in their time).

8 years on, they were still a massive customer, the service had spread to multiple divisions and people became advocates for the service, both within the organisation and outside of it.

That story for me, typifies the power of providing great service, and that is what I want to instil in you, through habit forming topics which you will have the joy of practising over the coming weeks and months. Get it right and it's tremendously rewarding.

> I felt it important to note, that after that moment back in 2012, the software's sending routines were re-engineered and for many years, Customer Thermometer has continued to process thousands of emails each day without incident!

Vocabulary

Because there are so many titles for people involved in the helpdesk world, I have tried to keep the language simple. I refer to an agent, throughout, which is interchangeable with operator, technician, engineer, team member, representative or whatever phrase refers to someone customer facing in your organisation.

Helpdesk could also mean service desk, internal support desk, shared services, IT support, customer service team, customer support or any other department dealing with inbound queries. Helpdesk fits nicely with the word 'habits', which was a good enough reason for me to settle on it.

I refer mainly to 'customers' throughout the book. The term could equally refer to internal customers, prospects, subscribers, citizens, clients or consumers.

You'll see I refer to my previous business from time to time. I'm indebted to my experience founding and growing Customer Thermometer and my ex-business partner and good friend, Lindsay Willott. I learnt so much about the customer service world, how to get customer service right and saw first-hand how companies struggle with getting it right.

Finally, there are many examples of both good and bad customer service throughout. I deliberately obscure the names of the companies involved. It would be wrong to single them out as either good or bad proponents of customer service, when I could have easily chosen different examples to paint them in a different light.

Now I've got things into context, I hope you are up for creating some new habits. First, we need a simple framework.

The ACETS pyramid

Introducing the pyramid

Like any skill in life, you have to work at it. You can't wake up one morning and have everything you need at your fingertips. It takes time, it takes practice. It takes experience.

All skills have to be taught from the ground up. You have to build on a platform and get the basics in place before you can move up to the next level. You can't train a pilot to land a 747 successfully if they've not mastered the theory of flight and landed a Cessna 152 hundreds of times.

Every business book needs a good framework, because it helps readers to piece together a jigsaw of new ideas as well as the ability to put them into practice. Without a framework, without structure, it's much harder to explain how new ideas fit together and readers are much less likely to adopt them.

The ACETS (*pronounced 'Assets'*) pyramid provides you with a structure for your habit building. You can see the skills and habits you must master, before moving up the pyramid towards becoming a Helpdesk Superhero.

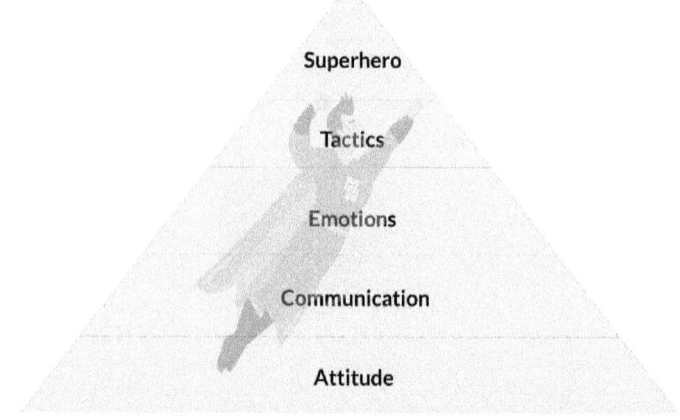

The ACETS pyramid

Attitude

Getting your attitude right, towards your role *and* your customers is the widest part of the pyramid. When you come into work with the wrong mindset, there's little point in remembering the rest of the Helpdesk Habits, as if your attitude is wrong, you will fail at the first hurdle and the pyramid will collapse.

Communications

The American personal development guru, Paul J Meyer said that *"communication is the key to personal and career success"*. He's right. If you can learn to communicate effectively (and I'm not talking about just spelling and grammar), then most other things will fall into place. This is why it's the second layer of the pyramid. Without these fundamental habits instilled, you can never truly master the art of customer service.

Emotions

Being a helpdesk agent often means taking on the skills of a counsellor and a therapist too. The general public (or your company's employees) will be challenging at times. People will often come across as irrational and emotional. Understanding how to read the signals and deal correctly with that emotion is critical. I'll also examine habits to handle your own emotions too, which can become frayed during pressurised days.

Tactics

With the fundamental habits in place, the pyramid can then continue to build by introducing tactics you can use every day, to make your life and your customers' lives easier. I want to encourage you to adopt the art of *'human* customer service'. By developing these tactical habits, you'll ensure customers are treated like royalty and will keep coming back for more.

Superhero habits

There's a lot to remember and practice in the first four layers of the pyramid, particularly if customer service doesn't come naturally to you. I hope by this point you'll have built more confidence in your role and will then have the capacity to excel. To use Seth Godin's trademark word, building a *remarkable* helpdesk requires Superhero habits. I aim to give you food for thought and the tools to help you and your team progress through the final layer of the pyramid.

That's enough preamble – it's time to get started.

ATTITUDE

"In the end, it's not going to matter how many breaths you took, but how many moments took your breath away"

– Xiong Sheng

Introduction

I think it's important to be honest and I recognise there is a possibility you're being asked to read this book, when a helpdesk environment isn't necessarily your passion. Instead, you're doing the job as a means to an end. If this *is* the case, then it's possible you're not going to be overly receptive to some of the ideas I put forward. I want to address this issue right away.

There are three types of people who will read this book.

- Someone who is in a temporary helpdesk position. They are working purely for the money, as a stop gap before a new start somewhere else.
- Someone who is in a helpdesk career, who perhaps doesn't enjoy it, feels stuck, but has commitments, so stays in their position.
- Someone who loves the helpdesk environment and enjoys their job.

If you're in the third category, this layer of the ACETS will act more as a reminder than a pep talk.

If you're in the first two categories, then my aim is to motivate and energise you. Do read on.

Everyone has to do things in life they don't always want to do. Your attitude towards your role will greatly affect your mental health, the way you're perceived and the opportunities which present themselves to you over the coming years.

This fundamental layer of the pyramid aims to put you into a positive mindset as you start each day.

Learn as much as you can

Doing something you don't enjoy for 8 hours/day, but feel you have to keep doing it, can go one of two ways. You can either make the most of that time (as you won't get it back) or, you can approach it as a chore, clock watch, focus your energies on leaving at the end of the day and doing the bare minimum.

I'm pragmatic – I know that the latter is tempting. I know that's the easy route to follow. I also know it's not sustainable. Eventually you will lose, your company will lose and the customers you're helping will lose too. Win-win is a much better equation. Let's look at some ways of creating an improved mindset.

If you are using this part of your career as a stepping stone. Think about what you could learn from every interaction. You are dealing with the 'general public' which is a crazy, unpredictable thing. Manning our chat service for days on end introduced me to a very strange cross-section of the world's population! You never know who's going to come through next via phone or email.

Every person has a different personality and set of needs, which means you have a tremendous opportunity to learn through *every* interaction. Human psychology is fascinating and you're in the privileged position of being paid to engage in a continuous daily experiment of how to deal with people.

The skills you will learn if you truly embrace this time and have the right attitude towards it are applicable to every role you'll ever take in the future. If you sit in management meetings in years to come, you'll watch the dynamics in the room and have a better understanding of what's going on, because of what you're learning today.

Empathy and rapport are vital tools of any job. You are currently in the best possible classroom to learn and hone your skills each day, via 100's or even 1000's of people during your time in the role.

> *"Leadership and learning are indispensable to each other."*
> John F. Kennedy

If you're not learning, you're not moving forward, and so develop the habit of considering this role, not, as a means to an end, but as a chance to further yourself ... as a chance to develop new skills.

Mastering people skills is the single most important characteristic for getting ahead in life.

Let's also not forget the subject matter skills that you are developing, to perform the role. Whether it's 3rd line IT support, hotel reservations or online banking, you are picking up valuable industry-related skills and experience.

Trigger > routine > reward

Bad day in the office > focus on leaving > going home

Bad day in the office > focus on learning > personal development

Remember Newton's 3rd Law

Time is our most precious asset. You can earn more money, you can buy more things, but short of being Marty McFly, you can't claw back time.

Remember that.

Every morning.

Make each day count.

Use your journey to work as your habit trigger. Remind yourself that you're going to make the most of the next 8 hours, as once they're gone, they're gone. Remind yourself that those hours are a finite resource and you're going to do everything in your power to make them great for yourself, your customers and the people around you.

Consider the alternative.

You could be wishing each day away and living purely for the weekend and holidays. This is a habit you really don't want to get into. This will mean the journey to work, will be spent dreading the next 8 hours, hoping each one speeds by as quickly as possible. You'll miss the opportunities to learn, to grow and do a non-remarkable job for the customers and people around you.

Really think about those two scenarios. Which one is more like you? Be honest.

Newton's 3rd law is a concept which I've experimented with for years. Let me remind you of the definition:

> "For every action, there is an equal and opposite reaction."

No doubt you're now having flashbacks to science lessons? This fundamental law of Physics absolutely applies to real life too.

A good friend of mine reminded me of this law over 10 years ago, and I've lived by it ever since. Let me explain.

If you take action, if you interact with your colleagues, if you have the right attitude, if you form great relationships with customers, if you add value to people's days, if you embrace what you're learning, then there *will be* some kind of reaction.

Quite often, the reaction you get, isn't the one you're expecting. Sometimes it's tangential, sometimes it's not going to benefit you directly. There *will* be a reaction though. The more action you take, the more there will be reaction. That reaction will end up furthering yourself, your career and your life, particularly when those actions are consistent. They then become compounded.

The opposite also applies. People who take no action, who sit around waiting for something to happen, yet still expect reaction and for good things to happen to them, are generally disappointed.

In my days before Customer Thermometer, I built and sold a couple of marketing and video agencies.

I built the website, I created a well-received and relevant offering, however, unless I got proactive, all I had (initially) was a shop window. I needed to remind myself, regularly of Newton's 3rd Law.

A personal experience

My favourite example of putting this into practice was a single email I sent to a renowned Australian Internet marketer. He had huge influence, had got into the Internet world early and was clearly wealthy. If I'm honest, I was slightly in awe of him and had questioned whether he would listen to little-old-me, over in the UK.

I had followed his every move for a couple of years and I could see he had a need for the video service I was offering at the time. After much thought, I sent one very carefully worded email. I remember having that nervous feeling when I hit the send button.

He responded positively within 24 hours. I was absolutely thrilled.

We spoke. We planned. I learned fast. I made two memorable trips to Australia, did a lot of filming, developed courses and through our partnership made a lot of money. I also was introduced to 20 of his like-minded colleagues and still have relationships with many of them today.

The alternative was *not* sending the email ... *not* being proactive ... *not* having that positive attitude ... *not* taking action.

That's not for me. I hope it's not for you either.

> # Trigger > routine > reward
>
> *Wanting to get ahead > wait for it to happen > no effort required*
>
> **Wanting to get ahead > taking action > unexpected reactions**

Have a wider purpose

I am borrowing the title of this topic from the ex-CEO of a CRM app called Highrise, owned by Basecamp. Nathan Kontky is well known in the SaaS world and wrote a post back in 2017 called What's my purpose. [Search: *signalvnoise my purpose*] It's thought provoking.

He talks about the Mayo Clinic, a US healthcare organisation, spread across three states. Their janitorial department is renowned for excellent hygiene.

When Iris Cowger, a janitor there, was asked to describe her role. She could have answered "I am part of the team that cleans the hospital". Instead she answered,

> *"We're not just cleaning rooms. We're saving lives".*

Yes, she cleans for a living, but her perspective on her job title and her attitude towards it are completely different, which provide her with motivation every day.

Everyone needs a purpose – a reason to get out of bed in the morning. I've seen people around me become a shadow of their former selves without purpose in their lives. Understanding where you're heading in life or even over the next few months will melt away stresses and anxieties. Instead, with purpose, you'll feel alive, you'll feel energised and you'll have focus too.

Whether your purpose is work related, outside of work or a combination of the two doesn't matter. What matters is that you have one.

If you struggle with your role, just like Iris above, develop the habit of elevating its purpose to something more meaningful, to help you to engage with it more fully.

Virgin Atlantic – creators of memories

Virgin Atlantic staff are trained to think of themselves as 'creators of memories', where they use the mantra of "brilliant basics, and magic touches".

Their training programmes embrace feedback and helps its cabin crew to adopt their purpose:

> *"I am not just a member of the on-board crew, delivering a meal service, I am a creator of great memories, for my on-board friends."*

Maybe they are both extreme examples, but if you're struggling with your attitude, could you come up with a similar approach? Could you find your actual purpose? A temporary purpose is fine. Nothing lasts forever. "My purpose is to improve my customers' days" is a good starting point.

My purpose

If you're looking for inspiration, I'm happy to share my purpose (at this particular moment in my life). I'm now looking to capitalise on what I've learnt over the last 20 years and help others to change.

My business is going to develop both paid for and not for profit courses for people who want to develop great habits across various niches. If I can make a difference to a few lives through my experiences, then I'm very happy and am living with purpose.

Trigger > routine > reward

Seeking more meaning > unfulfilled at work > something will turn up

Seeking a meaningful life > change of attitude > fulfilment

The service recovery paradox

I opened this book with a catastrophic failure (catastrophic as far as I was concerned at the time). Something went seriously wrong during the early days of our business. Our biggest customer at the time was angry, frustrated and embarrassed. As I mentioned, our diligence saw us through. At the heart of that diligence however was honesty. We were completely transparent about the problem. The customer didn't need to know everything, but they demanded answers (quite rightly), and we provided them.

Mistakes happen all the time in business. It's part of life. Whilst the immediate effect and impact may not be great, customers generally understand that things do go wrong.

> *What* you do to fix an issue and *how* you react to it, is what really matters.

The service recovery paradox is a concept I've talked about endlessly for the last 8 years. When it was first pointed out to me graphically, it made a big impact on my thinking.

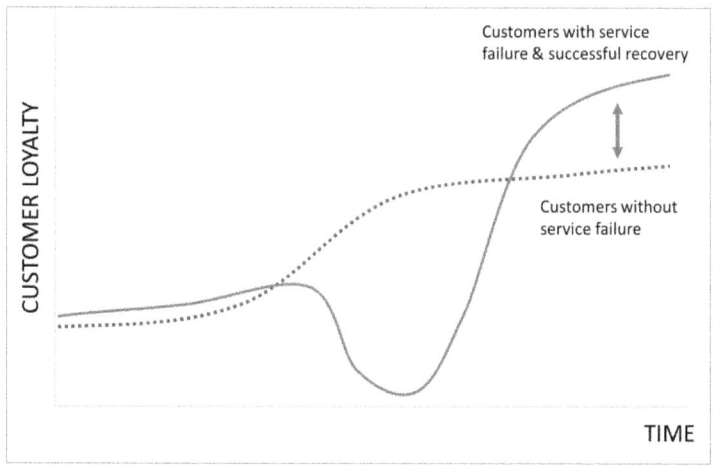

The service recovery paradox

The service recovery paradox states that, if you deal with a customer problem successfully, that customer is likely to be *more* loyal to you over time.

Let me rephrase that, for impact ... If a customer has a service failure and you resolve that failure in a professional manner to a customer's satisfaction, that customer will talk about you more, refer you more and become more loyal to your company over time!

It's an extraordinary concept and is absolutely true. Think about the human psyche for a moment.

If someone helps you out of a difficult situation (regardless of whether they've caused the problem in the first place) you then feel indebted to them. Your gratitude knows no bounds - it's human nature at its finest.

Here's an example I overheard a conversation in a coffee shop recently. Let me summarise it:

"I ordered a new screwdriver set, which arrived this morning – the case was cracked – one of the screwdrivers was missing.

I spent two mins on their chat, and a new one arrived the next day – I didn't even have to post the broken one back!

I'm really impressed with ScrewdriversRUs.com – I'd definitely use them again."

This is the service recovery paradox at work. A story has been told, a referral made, and the customer delighted. I suspect a great review was left in the relevant places too.

The opposite situation could have applied. ScrewdriversRUs could have blamed the courier company and a standoff would have ensued. Customer service then tells you to call the courier. The courier then says it was signed for. The consumer (unless they've real patience) realises it's a write off and it's not worth spending the time on it.

You as an agent have a part to play here. Whilst your company will have a policy on replacements and bigger incidents, there will be minor issues where something has gone wrong. Maybe a colleague hasn't returned a call or responded as they'd promised? Maybe you're at fault for your website displaying out of date information?

If you as a business are to blame, accept it, graciously and then go out of your way to fix the issue.

The way you accept that blame is important. Don't accept it with a "but", don't accept it with a "well, it's not really our fault". Choose your words wisely.

Recognise that problems will always occur in business. Also recognise, it's *how* you fix those problems, which is what really matters.

Trigger > routine > reward

Failure occurs > standard customer service > home on time

Failure occurs > remarkable, go out of your way customer service > delighted customer & personal fulfilment

Just smile

Before you dismiss this topic and flick to the next one, give me a chance to explain myself. Until I started to research this area, I was dismissive too. It turns out though, smiling can have both physiological and psychological effects. It can also make you better at your job - so please read on.

Developing the habit of smiling whilst having conversations does two things - it helps you as the agent to deliver your messages more effectively. Your smile can also be detected by the customer on the end of the phone.

Really?

Studies have shown that if you sit two agents back to back and one talks, the other listens, they can normally tell whether an agent is smiling and sat upright.

Smiling is good for you

If you're not sold on the benefits of smiling for your customers, this practice can also benefit your health.

In various studies, including one by the University of Kansas in 2012, experiments have revealed that smiling reduces stress. They proved heart rates and stress recovery were faster with candidates who smiled. In addition, it's been shown that smiling can retrain your brain, which is naturally negative, due to its inherent defence mechanisms, into a more positive space. You can actually help to encourage positive thinking patterns through smiling, which has to be a good thing.

It doesn't stop there, scientists have also discovered that your thoughts and mood have a direct effect on your cell function. When we smile, our cells become less rigid! This physical relaxation helps to combat the stress-induced mutations which go on to cause serious illness.

If you're in any doubt of the science of a customer responding to a smile, even over the phone, neuroscientist, Marco Iacoboni states we all possess 'mirror neurons'. When you see or 'feel' someone smiling, our "mirror neurons initiate a cascade of neural activity, that evokes the feeling we typically associate with a smile". Customers will subconsciously feel your smile through your words and timbre of your voice and respond accordingly.

I've yet to find any research which backs up these findings when using the written word, however I'm smiling right now, and it feels good ☺ , so what do you have to lose by trying it out?

Linked to the effect of smiling, many people prefer to stand up when talking on the phone. The physiological act of standing tall and straight may help you to come across as more confident.

Use a mirror

This maybe one of the more extreme habits I'm prescribing, however once again, I've read a lot to say that this technique works for both increasing CSAT scores and closing sales. Seeing your reflection stops any unconscious negative acts bringing down your energy.

Ask a colleague to place a mirror in front of you when you next make a call. Perhaps in the middle of it, just when you're not expecting it. Focus on your reflection. Focus on your eyes, your smile and adjust accordingly. Feel the difference it makes to your attitude.

You can use a mirror to check you're really present on the call or the task you're meant to be focusing on. Are you simultaneously checking your phone, your email or multitasking in other ways and so not focusing on the customer you're dealing with right now? A mirror can act as a warning to ensure you're giving your full attention to the task at hand.

You can also spot whether you're getting emotional. Are you getting angry or frustrated in response to a conversation? You're more likely to notice these emotions, if you're staring back at yourself and so can use the visual cues to adjust your temperament.

I know watching your reflection to check your mood sounds a little like witchcraft and you might be shaking your head at me right now. Give it a try though – you've nothing to lose. With or without the mirror, smiling certainly works – you've no reason to doubt me there!

It's time to lay down the challenge of turning smiling and 'attitude checking' into your next daily habit.

Trigger > routine > reward

Day of fluctuating emotion > carry on as usual > it's what I always do

Day of fluctuating emotion > remind yourself to smile, regularly > feel the endorphins flow!

Honesty is the best policy

This topic title isn't taken from your mum and dad. In fact, it's an original quote by Benjamin Franklin.

Honesty on the helpdesk should be a given. Emails are logged, details are shared, calls are recorded. Being deliberately dishonest with customers to make your day slightly easier is always going to catch up with you. Let's assume that's not in your psyche.

There are degrees of honesty however.

Qualification the right way

A customer always deserves honesty when making decisions around features of a specific service. This applies particularly to software.

"I need to have separate access for a colleague".

"I need the report emailed hourly."

"I need to have everything on the same bill".

With software, there are often different options available for the user to perform similar tasks.

Having the right attitude towards qualifying that customer in or out is important. Honest qualification as opposed to sneaky sales tactics will ensure a lengthy relationship.

An honest approach, particularly when breaking bad news is more palatable with explanation attached to it.

"No, I'm afraid the service doesn't offer the facility for hourly reports ..."

It's then often good to insert a rationale here ...

"We don't believe in bombarding customers with emails, as it's just not an efficient way to work ..."

The final thing to do in this type of situation would be to offer an alternative, assuming there is one …

"The service does have an API however, and many of our customers connect their widget service directly, and the information can be transferred seamlessly every minute. This may be a good option for you?"

Use this 'feature decision' trigger to switch in your honest qualification habit at this point.

The final part of this qualification dialogue would be to find out what they are *really* looking to do …

"If not, maybe drop me a line back, explaining exactly what you're looking to achieve, and I can see if there's a better option for you?"

Recommending competitors

In some cases, there will be no option at all and the customer simply won't be able to achieve what they're looking for with your service. If that feature is at the core of what they need, I believe it's then right to recommend an alternative service. Be honest – if you are certain you can't help them directly and have effectively qualified them out, then help them *indirectly*.

> Use your industry knowledge to recommend something that *will* work for them.

Controversial? I don't think so.

If they'd bought the service based on your advice, they would cancel soon. They'd have caused problems for the duration of their almost certain short tenure. You literally have nothing to lose by doing the right thing and recommending a competitor.

If their request is a small annoyance to them, and yet they love the service in other ways, then you should encourage them to raise a feature request. Again here, honesty is good in your response back to the customer. Logging a feature request doesn't mean the feature will exist soon, it's simply that you as a business will record their wishes and prioritise it.

Make sure you actually add it to the list too, don't say you will and then let it disappear into the ether – that benefits no one!

Money, money, money

There is nothing worse than mismatched expectations around pricing. If a customer ends up surprised, because of their lack of understanding around pricing, then difficult conversations will need to be had.

Tricking customers, misleading customers or 'forgetting' to mention charges to customers, in the hope they'll not spot them is not the right way to do business. I'd suggest you might be in the wrong place if that mentality is at the core of where you work. Assuming your company does have the right ethos, there's a big part for you to play when answering questions around pricing.

"We always like to be transparent. Did you realise that there would be an additional cost for that?"

Never assume a customer knows that they are on the right plan, have bought the right deal, are aware of additional charges, could potentially save money, or are on an out of date plan.

With longer term relationships, as opposed to one off sales, it's *unlikely* that a customer will be keeping an eye on the latest releases, features or offers. They won't necessarily know there's a discount they could be taking advantage of when they've raised their ticket. Where appropriate, take the opportunity to explain a new feature, update their plan, save them money or offer them a new deal.

Not only will you keep a customer longer if you proactively save them money or give them something additional, they will also tell their friends and become a promoter (in NPS parlance).

> **Trigger > routine > reward**
>
> *Qualification questions > sneaky sales tactics > temporary kudos*
>
> **Qualification questions > honest responses > long term success**

Apologise. The right way

Every agent will have to make an apology once in a while – when something has happened either inside or outside your control. You and your company's attitude to apologising needs to be the right one. Get it wrong and it can leave a really sour taste.

Acknowledge where the blame lies. If you've made a mistake, then own up to it – don't try and blame others. Making mistakes is part of any job and your attitude to dealing with them will be noticed by all around you, particularly customers, as we've seen with the Service Recovery Paradox.

> *"Mistakes are always forgivable if one has the courage to admit them."*
>
> Bruce Lee

Strike a balance. Apologies should always be sincere, however prostrating yourself in front of a customer isn't going to help them out of their situation. Being overly emotional or gushing with your words can start to backfire, so keep any apology to the point.

In verbal situations, sound like you mean it, as opposed to sounding like you're reading it from a script. When London Underground play the automated message over station speakers, proclaiming "*I'm sorry for the disruption to your service*", I tend to do the eye roll thing. Recorded message systems cannot be sorry for service disruptions, only people can be sorry. In the same way, "*Acme Widgets would like to apologise for the quality issue here,*" is also unacceptable. Acme Widgets is a legal entity and therefore cannot be apologetic.

"*Our operations team would like to apologise for the problems here. Our ops director, Sally Morgan would be happy to hear from you with any feedback,*" would be the best type of apology an organisation could make.

If you'd like a case study on how not to make apologies, [Search: *TSB bank apology*]. Their 2018 service failure and subsequent failure to deal with the fallout saw the demise of their CEO and 12,500 customers. Being honest with their customers from the outset would have seen a very different result.

Make it right

Any apology needs to be quickly followed with a remedy. Perhaps there is no remedy? Perhaps there's no information available internally on how to resolve it or explaining when it will be resolved? If that's the case, don't make it up. That will not help your customer either. Be honest. Explain you don't know how to fix the problem at that moment and that no one else in the company does either (ie you're not on your own here).

The only promise worth making in this situation is an update within a certain time period. That update might be via your website, it might be via email or it might be via a call back - whichever is most appropriate.

Promise a timescale - a customer will always want to know 'something' - they need to see progress, and an update *within a timescale* is at least 'something'. It may not placate the most irate of customers, but it will certainly help many.

Where answers are available, keep them succinct. Answers should be honest of course, but a customer probably doesn't need to know about upstream provider outages, breaking your SLA, causing latency issues and roundtrip delays.

Instead, this type of response works:

"The problem started at 11:07 this morning. Our engineers managed to return the service to normal within 17 mins. I know this must have caused you a difficult morning – we're going to be having a full investigation and will publish the results online within the week."

Typically, customers will never read the results of that investigation – but that's not the point. Some will read it. In addition, it shows you care as a business, are following through on your promises and are learning from a service issue, to stop something similar from happening in the future.

How not to 'apologise'

As I was writing this chapter, one of the UK's largest ISPs had a major network outage for 24 hours. To say their customers were unhappy, was an understatement. The biggest backlash came following the Tweet at the top of the image below where they stated the incident was resolved, without any form of apology.

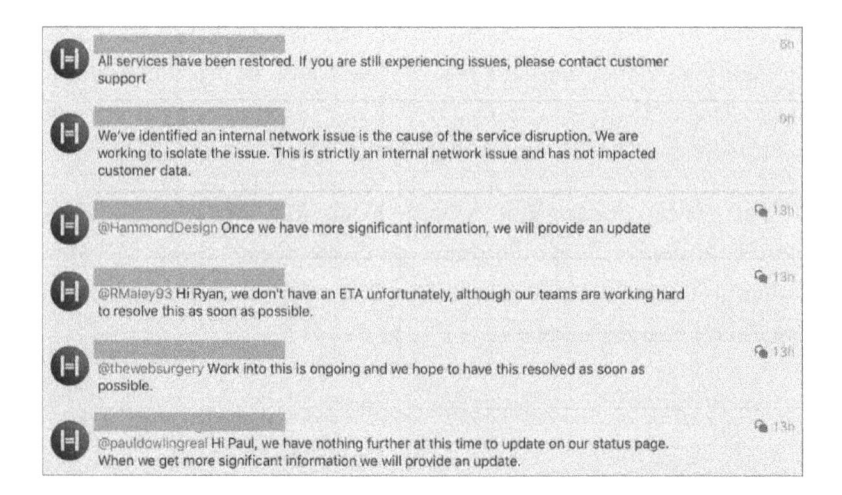

How not to apologise

They'd have been well advised to follow our example in the introduction to this book!

Think about the impact you could have with just 280 characters. Particularly if there's been a big incident. Have a process in place to have someone check social media output. In the heat of the moment or late at night in stressful situations, it's easy to make a situation worse, not better.

> Trigger > routine > reward
>
> *Service issue > no/poor apology > no embarrassment*
>
> **Service issue > confident apology > longer term, happier customers**

Be positive

If ever there was a habit to cultivate, it's the art of being positive.

The (now fugitive) Bikram Choudhury has talked about a negative attitude being nine times more powerful than a positive one. With the trend in mental health issues in the developed world, I'm inclined to agree.

You'll know if you're a naturally positive or negative person. Being honest, I started to become a bit of a *'moaner'* a few years ago. Small things would start to annoy me - normally because it meant wasting time (my biggest pet hate) and so rather than getting on with things, I started to moan to those around me. When it was pointed out to me, I was becoming a moaner, I was horrified. No one likes a moaner.

> I now have a laminated sign in my office,
> clearly stating - *'No moaning!'*

Despite that hiccup, I'd generally consider myself a positive person - I tend to see the best in people, trust everyone around me and make the best of situations. I think that helps me to write positively and to interact with customers in a positive way.

You may not put yourself in that camp. You may be in a situation right now, where you're feeling negative and it takes real effort to drag yourself away from those feelings. Hopefully some of the earlier topics will have helped overcome some of those feelings.

Understanding your prevailing outlook and attitude I think is helpful. It can help you adjust to situations. When you find yourself on the customer service front line, even the most positive of people can lapse into speaking and writing in a negative way. When you've bad news or no good answer to give, it's easy to come across as negative. Handily, it's easy to turn so many of these negative sounding phrases around. With practice, there are few situations that can't be made to be sound positive.

Learning to think positively and checking yourself when you get into difficult customer situations will automatically help with your writing or speech. It will take practice, but coming to work with the right mindset means that you'll start to spot those negative phrases and correct yourself. Triggering your 'Positive autopilot' mode is a brilliant habit and will brighten the days of the people around you, as well as your customers.

Your hopefully carefully chosen words, will be making or breaking a customer or prospect's day. They will help form that person's opinion of your company and determine whether they carry on or start doing business with you.

Subtle changes in language can make such a difference in perception, diffusion or retention. You'll find plenty of practical examples of this positivity in the Communications layer of the ACETS pyramid.

For now, I want you to really think about your mindset each day. Is it as positive as it could be? Are you generally seen as that negative person or is your outlook sunny? If in doubt – be brave. Have an honest conversation with a colleague – ask them whether you're a moaner, ask them if you brighten their day. It's a difficult conversation to have, but with everything to gain.

Trigger > routine > reward

Negative thoughts > moan > feel better for getting it off your chest

Negative thoughts > realise moaning doesn't help > gratitude for what you have around you

Be human. Be you

We are all surrounded by chat bots, AI and automation. I'm all for efficiency, but when I want to get something done and I'm short of time, I want to deal with a human who cares.

It turns out I'm not alone.

Genesys, a leading provider of customer service management software produced a fascinating report, "The cost of poor customer service" [Search: *genesys global survey*] to access it.

I'd like to highlight a single graphic from that report, which backs up my opening paragraph:

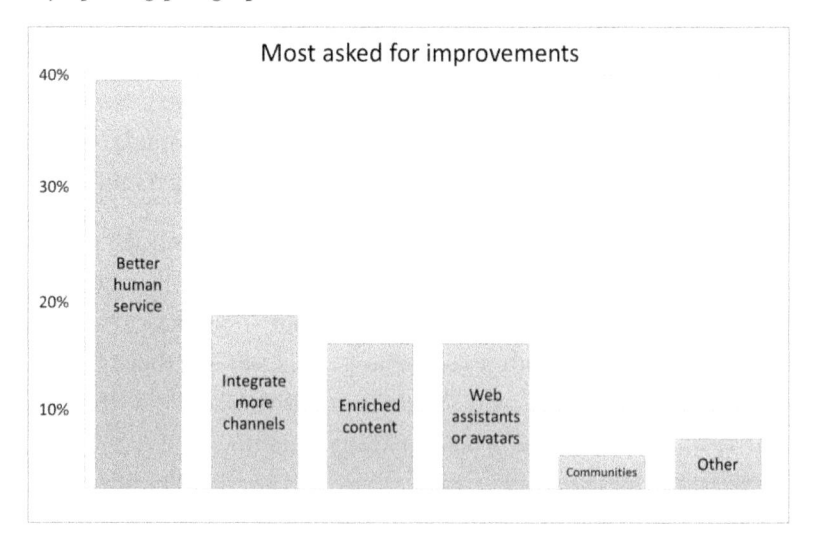

Most asked for improvements

- Better human service: ~38%
- Integrate more channels: ~17%
- Enriched content: ~13%
- Web assistants or avatars: ~13%
- Communities: ~5%
- Other: ~7%

Taken from the Genesys cost of poor customer service report

Whilst the exact definition of "better human service" is undefined in this survey, we can all take a guess at what it's indicating.

For me, it's all about having the right attitude (as a business and an individual) and it's why I wanted to finish the Attitude layer with this topic.

The Ministry of Magic

One of the proudest moments in my career saw me being part of Customer Thermometer's support team. I *was* the support team at the start of our journey. By the time I'd left, it was a fully-fledged team with more personality than you could shake a stick at.

I can say with absolute confidence that our support team was the reason many people bought our software tool. We differentiated by being human. We were proactive, thoughtful, helpful, would go out of our way to help both existing customers and prospects who needed help to buy.

I lost count of how many emails I'd receive from customers, thanking me for the support they'd received. It then dawned on me, that this type of support wasn't 'normal'. Expectations in the marketplace are low – which means *you* have a chance to shine and stand head and shoulders above your competition.

The Customer Thermometer helpdesk developed its own brand

Customer Thermometer could have been a faceless CSAT application which happily ticked along, doing its job, as software does. Instead, we became known for our service first and the tool second. We were not faceless, we were a software company with a personality – imagine that! Customer service actually became a feature of the service. Customers and prospects knew they'd get timely helpful responses and when being compared with another application which had similar functionality, we'd win a deal purely through personality.

That for me, sums up the definition of *human* customer service.

Plenty of other businesses have gone down this route. Famously Zappos is continuously in the news for its customer service prowess. [Search: *imgur trws6*] for a legendary example of a customer service email, which defies belief.

Good news spreads fast

When customer service becomes less robotic and more human, amazing things happen.

The UK supermarket, Sainsburys gained thousands of pounds worth of PR coverage in Jan 2012, when they turned tiger bread into giraffe bread, following a letter from a 3 year old girl.

A Netflix customer service chat agent raised the bar somewhat, by responding to a customer as a Star Trek captain. [Search: *netflix captain mike*]. Bizarrely, as a reward, this agent went on to meet Bill Shatner via a news report link up. His reaction makes for a great watch on YouTube.

Lego are no strangers to being human either. Their exchange with 7 year old Luka Apps is stuff of customer service folklore. Their simple exchange with agent, Richard, has generated 100's of references online and makes the Lego team look like superheroes. [Search: *luka apps lego*] and keep scrolling ...

So how can you have an effect?

I can provide examples of multinational companies creating good news stories all day long, however, lets relate this back to you and your helpdesk.

Your company will have its own personality. Where you're allowed to be 'you' - then make the most of it! You are unique - let your personality shine through when writing and speaking with customers. Be friendly, have a heart, be human. Using these traits doesn't stop you from being efficient and getting the job done. Instead, they improve how the message is delivered and received.

You need to know when it's appropriate to make a remark and when to reign it in. It takes confidence to have that personality. It will come with experience. If in doubt, always play it safe. The Emotion layer of the ACETS pyramid will help with this.

Human customer service doesn't just mean showing your personality, it can also mean going the extra mile, going out of your way to make it right for a customer. Whether it's meeting a customer at an airport with a steak [Search: *morton's steakhouse airport*] or Southwest airlines looking after a young passenger [Search: *southwest garrick*] you too can take the opportunity to give a customer 110% in your replies and interaction with them.

Be remembered. Be remarkable. Be human.

If you feel your company wouldn't allow you this type of free reign, show your helpdesk manager this topic, or give them my contact details and I'll persuade them.

Trigger > routine > reward

A normal day > standard responses > following procedure, doing my job

A normal day > personality + extra mile > sense of fulfilment

COMMUNICATIONS

"What's the greatest advice I can give? Develop excellent communication skills."

- Julie Sweet, CEO, Accenture, N America

Introduction

So many recruiters of customer service agents talk about how important it is to be able to write well.

> *"We look for people that are good writers ... your ability to write well directly relates to how effective you are at being able to interact with the rest of your team."*
>
> Chase Clemons, Basecamp support

Excelling at spelling and grammar requires a different skillset to being a great communicator. Getting a message across is one thing. Delivering it in a professional, well written style, is another. Both however, are equally important to practice and improve.

Having seen the effect a positive Attitude can have, it's now time to focus on the Communication habits you need to become an exceptional customer service agent. This is the next layer in the Helpdesk Habits ACETS pyramid and is fundamental to delighting customers.

Having recruited dozens of people over the years, in both a freelance and full time capacity, my initial impressions are normally formed by introductory emails. The individual may have been proactive and written directly, or has responded to a request. It always amazes me just how little care people generally take in their first response.

> They just don't seem to appreciate the impact their writing will have on the receiver of the email.

I do understand that not everyone enjoyed their grammar lessons at school. I also appreciate that not everyone prides themselves on their spelling. However, with the tools available at our finger tips today, there is absolutely no excuse for not getting this right.

You need to develop habits to make the right first impression with a customer. You then need to work at making each subsequent impression count too.

Customer service communication is like a great referee during any sporting occasion. If they are doing their job well, no one notices they are there. In the same way, few people will proactively comment on brilliantly formed sentences and perfect spelling.

The opposite applies. If a referee makes a glaring error, suddenly the spotlight will focus on their performance. If an already annoyed customer gets a poorly written, sloppy email response, then you as an agent are clearly not helping to resolve the situation in the best possible way. The spotlight will then fall on you.

Even if you are primarily phone-based, writing skills are still an important skill to get right. Not only will they enable you and your team to write coherent documentation, they also indicate you are a person who can think and communicate clearly.

Let's now look at how we can keep a spotlight on you, but for all the *right* reasons.

Spelling and grammar matter

You will already know if your spelling is naturally good. You'll know if you write well-structured sentences. You'll also know if you can handle apostrophe's.

I'll help you to answer the third point above – I'm hoping you've noticed something incorrect?

If spelling and grammar is something you pride yourself on, then feel free to move on to the next topic. If you recognise it's not one of your strengths, let's look at some of the habits you can develop to improve and help yourself.

Firstly, accept it's not a strength of yours. Secondly, appreciate that for many people, it absolutely does form an immediate and lasting impression of both you and the company you work for and therefore it's something you need to commit to improving.

Many helpdesk systems will have editing tools to help with spelling. If yours doesn't, then get into the habit of opening a separate browser window each day you start work. If you have doubts about how you've spelt something, don't ignore that feeling. Don't dismiss it. Go the extra mile. Get it right. Type the word into your browser, and let Google tell you whether it's right or wrong.

Keep an ongoing list of the words you continuously misspell. Let them sink in. Teach yourself. Don't just accept spelling isn't your thing – help yourself by taking small steps each day.

If there is no spell checker within your editor and you genuinely couldn't recognise whether a word might be spelt incorrectly, then where practical, ask a colleague to look over your responses, particularly those to important customers, where spelling could really matter.

Use the tools around you

Helpdesk editors can also help with sentence structure and grammar. This is a trickier skill to master as there's no right way, but there's normally multiple wrong ways! If your helpdesk tool doesn't help with grammar, open a copy of MS Word, paste in the sentence you're struggling with, highlight that phrase and press F7.

The Editor tool within Office365 has improved enormously over the years to help writers create better sentence structures. Sometimes you won't agree with it – but it will provide food for thought and alternatives to your way of writing.

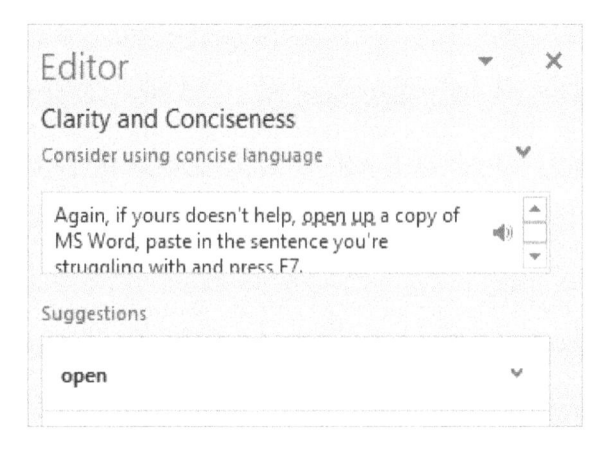

MS Word's grammar checker helped me to write this book

Get into the habit of looking at alternative sentence structures and slowly you will start to become more natural at writing. Make the most of the plethora of tools at your fingertips. There really is no excuse with today's technology all around you.

Use your personality

Don't be afraid to use your personality when writing responses. Always be you, where appropriate. I've talked about human customer service. Now's your opportunity to live it. Be creative with your writing. Choose your words carefully. Add humour where appropriate – aim to put a smile on a customer's face by not writing what they'd expect to hear. That's remarkable.

Apostrophes

If you struggle with the use of apostrophes, remember that an apostrophe is either used to replace a letter or letters (it's = it is) or it's used to express ownership (Mark's writing). There's just no excuse for getting this wrong.

In so many helpdesk roles, the only thing a customer can use to form an opinion of you, is your writing. You should always be aiming to create the best impression you possibly can, using just the power of words.

Trigger > routine > reward

About to hit send > no diligence > speedy responses, more tickets answered

About to hit send > take time to check > better responses, happier customers

---

Use short sentences

Writing a book is quite different to forming ticket responses and so before you pick up your keyboard to rant at me, *I'm allowed to use longer sentences, if I wish* 😏.

With ticket responses, your aim should be to use as few words as possible in any response, whilst retaining the 'being human' aspect of the communication.

More words can provoke more questions. More words can confuse. More words can mean a customer doesn't read them *all*. So often people will skim responses, to get to the answer they think they're looking for. Imagine your customer is running for a train and looking at their mobile device to get the information they need. If the answer is buried within reams of text, that won't be helpful and could even cause an additional request. I'm often guilty of not reading something properly the first time. Are you?

Keeping sentences short is a good habit to get into.

> Try to communicate one concept at a time.

Don't try to include too much information in a single sentence, or you will make the email response much harder to read and the customer is less likely to see the answer if they're skimming their email, in a rush on their mobile device.

See what I did in that paragraph?

One tip I was taught many years ago by a mentor, was to read an email back before sending, to see how many extraneous words you can remove from it, whilst keeping the meaning the same, but without sounding rude.

It's a good habit to double check emails before you send them back to customers, to see how many words you could remove.

Always check emails for unnecessary words.

See what I did in those last three paragraphs?

Of course, there's always a balance. We need to remember all of the other ACETS habits too! Empathy, warmth etc need to be woven in. Always try to get the balance right. All that said, I hope the power of "less is more" is clear to see.

Trigger > routine > reward

Checking a response > verbose writing > another comprehensive response sent

Checking a response > check for extraneous words > clearer responses, happier customers

Link externally

Keeping on the theme of brevity, many of my Customer Thermometer support days involved making explanations of how specific features worked. It was all too easy to start writing lengthy responses and to get into complexities quickly.

"If you click the link on the main menu and scroll down and then click the drop down ..."

Not only does this start to make email responses long and tedious to read, they are also difficult to write. Quite often, you'll find yourself writing the same set of instructions time and again.

I talk about canned responses in the Superhero Habits layer of the ACETS pyramid. The concept of linking externally applies to canned responses too.

A good helpdesk will have a wealth of self-serve information sat behind it – ready for customers to read and take action with. Not only can customers use it to self-serve, *you* can use those same assets to help them directly too.

Get familiar with what's available. Based on your experiences, volunteer to amend / input and add new sections, based on the questions you receive. Once you're aware of the assets available to you, it will allow you to create better responses and improve your response times too, as you're not spending precious minutes reinventing the wheel with your responses every time.

Always focus on brevity. If you find yourself starting to write a lengthy, detailed response, use this as your habit trigger to shorten and link out.

Here's an example of a response which *could* have become lengthy and potentially contain screenshots and a detailed set of instructions.

Look how simple it is to avoid that from happening, whilst still giving the customer exactly what they need.

____

Thanks for your email.

Absolutely! You can make background colour changes to the widget in your settings screen.

It's simple to do. You can find a full explanation here. [Link to user guide].

Best wishes,
Mark

____

If your company doesn't already have a user guide / knowledgebase / self-help tool online, then you need to talk to your manager! It's one of the most important tools for any helpdesk to have in place and will save both agents and customers valuable hours.

Be inspired by the best example of a knowledgebase I know. Visit https://www.customerthermometer.com/user-guide/

Trigger > routine > reward

Lengthy response > hit send > comprehensive must be good

Lengthy response > how can I shorten with links? > less is more

Lay it out

How a written response looks to a customer, really helps in their interpretation and understanding of it.

Often a customer will ask two or more questions within a single ticket – it could almost read as a train of thought, as opposed to separately posed questions. You need to practice the art of ensuring that each question is answered separately and double checking you've ticked off all questions within the ticket.

When you've figured out what actually needs to be answered, it's time to trigger your lay it out habit. You must remind yourself that it's rare a customer will be sat with a coffee in front of a 1920 x 1080 screen with no distractions around them. More often than not, customers will be reading responses on mobile devices, between tasks or whilst running for a train. It's really important to develop the habit of making each response as clear as possible.

Clarity is essential

Whilst I recommend mirroring during this programme, this could be the one time not to mimic an inbound requestor's writing. It's time to use the tools available to you to lay out your response for maximum clarity and effect. This is assuming your Helpdesk tool editor allows for this.

Firstly, use paragraph spacing - space out your sentences sensibly - let them breathe. Use the white space of the page to make the layout as simple to read as possible. Running paragraphs or sentences together as we'll see shortly, means customers can miss points and will therefore potentially ask for clarification, despite the fact you'd already provided the answers.

Secondly, go old school - use bullet points to establish points separately. This format will make each point easy to read and understand. Where appropriate, use bold or underline text too, to emphasis the most important points within the ticket. Differing styles like this make reading a response easy on the eye and this can be a real advantage on a small, mobile screen.

Hi Matthew,

You can certainly end your contract at any time you like. There's no commitment once you get started. You'll see the trial button on the main homepage, which is where you can create an account and the trial will last 28 days. If you do need more time though – let us know, we'll be happy to help. Our support team is here for you during work hours – just drop us a line and we'll get right back you.

Best wishes,
Mark

Before sending a response, always make sure you read it back. If it starts to run together and is hard work to interpret, use this to trigger this 'lay it out' habit and see whether you can find a better approach. Effort required is minimal. Customer impact is huge. It makes you look more professional as an organisation too.

Here's my alternative approach, using the techniques I've already talked about:

Hi Matthew,

Thanks for your questions.

- Our service has no commitment – cancel any time. The details are here. [LINK]
- To get started, you can grab a trial here [LINK]
- Trials last 28 days, but we're happy to extend if you drop us a line.
- Our support hours are 9-5 EST.

If you need anything else – please don't hesitate to write back – it'd be great to have you on board!

Best wishes,
Mark

Can you see the difference some simple tweaks to the layout makes?

In addition, I'm also layering on the previous habit, around 'linking out'. You can see how easy it is to add additional information, from your user guide, to keep the email brief and therefore easy to interpret. All questions have been answered separately too.

Adding bullet points, text formatting and correct paragraph spacing is an underused technique in my experience and adds real value to that busy customer running for a train.

Don't be afraid to use the bullet point button. It's an underused format and adds real value to that busy customer running for a train.

Trigger > routine > reward

Single paragraph response > hit send > another response answered

Single paragraph response > how could I use bullets and spacing? > clearer customer responses, less replies

Tone of voice

The beauty of working in our industry, is that you get the privilege of dealing with every type of person imaginable. This means you have been given the best natural training ground for lessons in mirroring tone.

> I like to think of tone as rapport,
> but using the written word.

Where a customer is informal towards you, take their lead and respond informally providing that fits with your company's culture. As always, keep a balance. Don't ever let your informality go too far.

The opposite applies. When someone comes across as formal, then you must respect that. Addressing them as 'Mr' or 'Mrs' may feel old fashioned, but if in doubt, then mirror their style. They will appreciate your tone. Brevity and clarity should become even more of a focus with a formal customer.

Use of tone can be taken a step further, as you become more confident of your customer relationships.

Adding elements of humour or being slightly tongue in cheek is potentially dangerous but can reap huge dividends when used correctly. Do be very wary of this in a corporate environment and always respect your company's wishes.

Throwing in "*LOLs*" followed by a "*Yours sincerely*" is clearly never going to be a great piece of writing – so make sure you keep your writing consistent.

With a smaller business, customers can often become more familiar with you, this more informal tone can be quite a magical thing. It can make a customer's day. You and your business could start to become truly memorable (and referable). You will also become known for your outstanding customer service.

Customer Thermometer managed to create that sort of environment. We injected real personality into our response writing and set ourselves apart from the crowd. The effect was incredible. We were no longer another soulless software company, we were known for having a real human touch.

Emoji

I'm sure the Egyptians are smiling somewhere now, as pictorial representations have crept into our language over the last few years, in the form of emoji 😌

Like them or not, when MS Word adds them automatically to manuscripts, you know they are part of our language and culture for years to come.

That said, some customers won't appreciate you using them. Others however, will be happy to see them spread liberally around a response. Sense the tone. Think about the customer and the situation and if it makes sense, find that emoji to use. There are some great Chrome extensions to help select them [Search: *emoji chrome extension*].

The **EMOJIONE** chrome extension

Foreign language

Recognise too, whether a customer has *your* language as *their* native language. If they don't – then you'll need to adjust your tone accordingly. Avoid slang. Avoid other colloquial language and keep your sentences simple.

Writing this reminds me of my Dad talking to overseas customers on the phone at home in the early 80's. Whatever you do, don't resort to talking more loudly (sometimes shouting in fact), so that the customer understands ☺.

You'll find more around tone in the Emotions layer of the ACETS pyramid.

Trigger > routine > reward

Customer conversation > use standard wording > another response answered

Customer conversation > adapt words to *their* tone > speaking *their* language will resonate with them, relationships develop

Phrase correctly

You can make such a difference to a response by choosing words with more care, or even rearranging the order they appear in.

For example, compare:

"You have to logout first"

with ...

"Logging out (top right of the menu bar) will help to solve that issue."

That's a deliberately stark example to illustrate a point. You may have a particular writing style and not even realise it.

My wife will naturally write the first option above – she *can* come across as very direct and without warmth. She is self-aware though and is always careful with phrasing – even when writing texts to friends. She will always reread a text before sending it and often rewrite it. She doesn't mean to be cold, she just naturally writes *to the point* as she's not one to waste people's time and likes to get things done. She's also had 25 years in a corporate environment, so that might help explain her style!

You may naturally write in a direct way. Or, you may be more like me, naturally verbose if not reigned in and checked.

> Everyone has a natural style and it's important to figure out what yours is. Be cognisant of it and then counteract it, where necessary.

Sometimes providing a direct response is the best approach. In a customer service environment, it *might* not be.

Let's look at another example:

"Yes, we can refund that charge" ...

... is one possible response.

"That charge will be refunded right away and will show in your account within 3 working days" ...

... is a better one.

Be more accountable

Here's another example. Might you be guilty of using this phrase?

"That must be frustrating."

It sounds innocuous enough doesn't it? You're showing empathy - you're saying to the customer, that you understand, what could be wrong?

"I can understand how frustrating that must be."

A tiny change in the phrasing makes such a difference - it shows real empathy now - it's making it personal - it's showing that you really care, because you're putting yourself into the shoes of the frustrated customer.

I talk about 'getting personal' later in the book. It's a good moment to bring it up here too. So often, we lapse into referring to a faceless organisation - referring to the 'team' or a 'colleague' or a 'department'. A customer's heart sinks when they hear this kind of phrasing, as it indicates rightly or wrongly that this enquiry may head into the 'corporate black hole'.

Writing or saying something like

"The team will resolve this issue soon"

in response to an inbound issue doesn't make a customer's day. If anything, it ruins it. It sounds like you're being fobbed off.

A small amount of thought (assuming it's based on accurate facts) can make this response so much more helpful to a customer:

"I am working with my resolution team to get this issued resolved for you as soon as possible. I'll update you within 24 hours".

This is much more specific and accountable and gives the impression to the customer *you* are owning the issue. Make sure you do 😅.

Phrasing bad news

In experiments, people who are given bad news first, are more likely to feel better about what they were told. People who are given bad news last, are typically more motivated to act on the news. So, what does that mean to us as agents? How can we act on this?

There's a well-known type of sandwich used to describe the best way of delivering bad news. Start and end with the good news, and sandwich that with the bad news in the middle of the conversation.

"Hi Charlotte, we've got one of our most experienced engineers on the way to your site right now.

Unfortunately, he has been delayed on the previous job and so he's going to be a couple of hours late.

We'd like to offer you a discount on your bill though, to apologise for the inconvenience."

Trigger > routine > reward

Customer response > standard phrasing > another ticket answered

Customer response > how can I make this response more helpful through simple word changes? > happier customers

Make it your job

I can feel you 'eye rolling' at the thought of someone saying that to you, particularly after you've been on hold for 30 mins. There's nothing worse. Remember that feeling. Make sure you don't do it to your customers.

We all have processes. We all have procedures and sign off levels and authorisations. That's the way it should be for a viable business to function. The secret is to not let those boundaries be apparent to customers.

The customer doesn't care whether you have the authority, whether you're not in that department, whether the system won't let you do that or whether the 'computer says no.' [YouTube Search: *computer says no*]!

Learning from a UK bank

Let's remember that positive mindset I talked about in the Attitude layer of the ACETS pyramid. You're being asked something of you which you can't personally deal with. How could you respond? First Direct bank do this brilliantly in the UK. You can only talk to the first line agents when you call initially. They will take you through security and then for more complex issues, will hand you over to an expert, quite brilliantly, every time.

> "Ok, to make an international bank transfer, I'll need to transfer you to a colleague, can you bear with me one moment?"... music on hold ... "Oh hi, [colleague name], I've Mr Copeman on the line – he'd like to make an international transfer ... Thank you [colleague name]. Hi Mr Copeman, I've your details on screen – how can I help?"

The experience is always so pleasant. You know you're not going to be asked for more security details and you aren't losing the time invested – it's just a continuation of a process with an expert. Hearing the handover is always so good too – they are passing ownership, as opposed to that sinking feeling of having to explain yourself once again to a different agent.

As a side note, I've been with First Direct for 25 years.

Politely deferring

Let's look at another scenario, this time with a ticket thread. It's a really common situation I've found myself dealing with many times over the years.

A customer writes to you *directly*, with an issue, as they have an existing relationship with you and know your email address. You've helped them in the past, they trust you and like you. Why wouldn't they go to you directly to get something done?!

Your process states that customers need to raise a ticket via the website to get support, or call a central number, so that it can be billed correctly and allocated to the right person.

A response to this type of inbound enquiry could be:

"I'm really sorry Lucy, but I can't answer your request directly – you'll need to raise a ticket via [URL]."

It's honest at least – and whilst the customer might understand, it'll leave them feeling a bit deflated with the situation. Firstly, you're making them do extra work. More importantly, there's a relationship at stake here and the personal service they hoped they were able to receive has just been taken away from them.

There's a better way to respond:

"Hi Lucy, good to hear from you.

To get your request actioned quickly and accurately, I've taken your request and raised a ticket for you. I'm not sure yet who will be dealing with it. It could be me!

So that we can best answer requests from you and your team, in the future, please can you raise a ticket via [URL]. It'll make sure the right expert deals with your request and you'll also be able to track its progress.

Hope all is well, and Tom is behaving himself!"

This type of positive response does three things:

- It keeps it personal – it makes Lucy feel like there's still a relationship there.
- It removes the headache of her raising that ticket this time round – you've done it for her.
- It educates her on the right way to make requests going forward and explains why the process exists.

This type of approach has always worked brilliantly for me. Turn this 'direct approach' trigger into a positive habit – maintain your relationships, but make the process work.

Trigger > routine > reward

That's not my job > put onus back on the customer > no longer your problem

That's not my job > make positive suggestions > customer feels like they've been helped

Hollow words and phrases

Wherever you're reading this book around the world, your country will have its own cultural nuances and many phrases you see every day are expected and necessary. Other phrases will make you squirm, regardless of your nationality.

It has always amazed me that so many superfluous words and hollow phrases are used within email threads and call centre scripts. I'm starting to see the same hollow phrases on chat services too - no doubt you will have noticed them too.

There's a simple test to use in your writing and speech - whether on the phone, chat or email.

> **Does this phrase sound automated?**

Does what you're saying or writing contribute anything to the conversation? If it doesn't, don't use it.

I will look at some examples of these hollow phrases over the next few topics and consider why they are such a detraction. For now, let's see what the impact of a few simple words can make.

Words to avoid

Take a look at the different scenarios below and the suggested responses:

Scenario 1:

Customer: *"I'd like to suggest a feature request"*

Agent: *"Thanks, but our development cycle is fixed now for the next six months."*

Using '*but*' or '*however*' after a '*thank you,*' '*yes*' or '*sorry*', immediately detracts from that preceding word. That tiny addition effectively says to the customer you're paying lip service to whatever they've just said.

You can convey the same message in a much more positive way, with a simple change ...

Agent: "*Thanks! I really appreciate you writing in. We review all feature requests regularly and make our development decisions every six months. You can subscribe to feature updates here ...*"

Agent: "*I'm really sorry, but no, we're not able to access that database*"

This is effectively an apology - which isn't needed. It is unfortunate for the customer - they can't get done what they need to, but they don't need this pointing out to them. They already know!

Agent: "*I'm afraid we're not able to access that database – it's really important we keep that data secure*".

Always be careful of being too apologetic. Be accurate with your facts, be sympathetic of the situation, but there's no need to labour the point.

Agent: "*Actually ...* "

It's easy to throw this word into a sentence. Be careful though - it can come across as negative. Often, it's used to correct a customer, whether verbally or written.

"*Actually, you can't upload a pdf ...*"

When used incorrectly, an agent can come across as superior and condescending.

'Actually' should become a trigger word for you. Always double check your usage and if need be, think about an alternative phrase, such as the one below.

"I'm not sure if you're aware, but you're not able to upload a pdf".

Develop that habit trigger when you start to write these troublesome words and always double check the context and whether there's a better way of constructing the sentence.

Agent: "*It's our policy ...* "

All companies have to have policies and procedures for them to operate profitably. They are only indirectly beneficial to customers and they certainly don't need to hear about them. The phrase itself can send shivers down the spine – it can be seen as an excuse to not get something done and makes you sound like you don't care.

Here's an alternative.

"One thing we could do for you is..."

Tell customers how you've resolved similar, difficult situations in the past – offer an alternative, rather than denying them something, due to policy. If you can't – read the topic on 'Delivering bad news.' Whatever you do, don't resort to policy!

Agent: *"That's dealt with by a different department"*.

The word 'department' seems innocuous enough doesn't it? However, consider changing that word, when you're tempted to use it. Instead, talk about referring to colleagues.

'Department' sounds impersonal – it makes you sound corporate and that if something gets passed there, it may get lost and overlooked.

Referring to colleagues sounds more human. Your customer will therefore feel like their enquiry is more likely to get dealt with.

Develop a habit trigger for when you begin to write those troublesome 'but', 'actually', 'department', 'policy', and similar, words. Always double check the context and whether there's a better way of constructing the sentence.

> **Trigger > routine > reward**
>
> *Negative sounding response > send anyway – one word change won't help> another ticket answered quickly*
>
> **Negative sounding response > check for hollowness > I've written the best possible response**

I'm going to continue down this path now, as it's such an important part of the Communications layer of our ACETS pyramid. Customers can spot insincerity and fake words from a distance and it's time to eradicate them.

The next few topics concentrate on rogue *phrases* which are creeping into the customer service lexicon and examines why they should be removed and replaced.

I'd be happy to assist you with this today

Bleurgh ...

This is now common at the start of online chat sessions. It makes my eyes literally roll.

An agent has just clicked "send initial chat template response", without thought or feeling. What makes this type of response particularly cringeworthy is when the initial chat input is a complaint, or you have a particularly emotional customer on the line. This canned response is simply not empathetic to the initial input.

If you're a regular user of a helpdesk's chat service - to see that phrase pop up every time you raise a request will eventually drive you to distraction, before you've even started chatting.

I think that's the problem with the rogue phrases I'm identifying in the Communications layer - customers crave empathy. They want to know they are being listened to and understood and that a real human (behind the façade of a chat room) genuinely wants to help them. They don't want a robotic type response. Using this specific phrase gets things off on the wrong foot.

How about using a more personal approach?

Customer: "Hi – please can you help me with order #139930 – it was delivered yesterday, and the packaging was damaged and now the widget is broken and unusable."

Agent: "I'd be happy to assist you with this today."

Now we've removed this rogue phrase from our automated responses, what's a better first response to greet the customer?

Agent: "Hi – I'm so sorry to hear that. Let me try to make this right for you asap. Could you confirm your surname please?"

This alternative demonstrates empathy and understanding and gets right down to business. No time wasting. No template. Immediately, the customer will feel like they're dealing with someone who cares and is going to help them. This type of agent response will also have a dramatic effect on the next input from the customer too.

If that agent goes on to resolve that situation (delivering a new widget in the morning), how many people will that customer tell?

> **Trigger > routine > reward**
>
> *Time to open a conversation > I'd be more than happy to assist you > I'm following the script*
>
> **Time to open a conversation > respond naturally > conversation begins well**

And so, these are the next 11 words to remove from your lexicon, automations and scripts with immediate effect. Let's look at some more ...

Give me a moment to look into that

I'm sure you've been on the receiving end of this phrase - whether on chat or the phone. Once again, customer service chat is particularly bad at the use of this hollow phrase, as it's quite often the first response back from an agent, following an initial request.

It's fine if it's followed quickly by word of explanation. Invariably it isn't, which means that for the first 5 mins of a chat - you're spending the time wondering if you're still connected.

That can't be right.

Customers just want to feel that they are being communicated with and that someone cares about their problem.

Setting expectations

If you need to go quiet to investigate an issue, let your customer know what's about to happen. Be clear - explain the plan. Tell them what you need to do (briefly) and explain that it's going to take a certain length of time. If it's going to be really challenging to get things resolved as it's a difficult issue, let them know it's going to take some time and perhaps offer to call or email back?

"*Give me a moment to look into that.*" ... Silence.

Alternatively ...

"*OK - I understand the issue you've come across. I need to access your account and check some of the settings - please can you bear with me - I'll update you within the next 3 mins*".

3 mins passes.

Always follow through with your timing. Don't let someone wait 5 minutes if you've promised 3 minutes - they'll start to become twitchy and lose faith you're still there.

"Sorry to keep you waiting – I'm almost done – I can see the issue – bear with me for another 5 mins and I'll update you again."

If you clearly signpost timings, on the other end of the line, your customer can be getting on with something else, knowing that their issue is being dealt with.

This is a much better alternative to wondering whether the agent has gone on a break.

Trigger > routine > reward

Need to investigate an issue > give me a moment to look into that > I believe I'm communicating

Need to investigate an issue > explain next steps with a timescale > customer feels fully kept in the loop

---

Using internal jargon

There's a topic called 'Never Assume' in the Superhero Habits layer, which is relevant here too. Internal jargon, technical assumptions, referring to internal systems and processes and talking as if the customer has been an integral part of your business for the last 5 years is a helpdesk crime of enormous proportions.

A personal experience

Earlier this year, I had to speak to a well-known white goods manufacturer. Our (very expensive, recently purchased) fridge freezer decided to stop cooling one night during a very hot summer. This was unknown to me, as the temperature gauge on the front of the fridge still showed the original, freezing temperatures. It was the equivalent of a fridge blue screen of death ...

Having eventually discovered a warm, defrosted freezer full of food and a fridge of limp lettuce, I did what any budding electrical engineer would do, I switched it on and off. Which fixed the problem. It started cooling again.

I then called them.

To save you from reading 3 days of transcript, I was *eventually* promised some vouchers for the ruined food.

Two weeks later, no vouchers had arrived. I called again, to be told (in great detail) how their systems wouldn't allow this request to be processed, because an engineer hadn't come out to visit. As there was no visit, there wasn't a job number assigned and so it was therefore impossible to have a voucher request processed. I even heard about internal names of systems too – I know a lot about this company's support now.

The computer literally said *"no"*.

I may have eye rolled. Again.

I was spending hours of my time, hearing about the limitations of this huge company's internal processes and systems. Believe me, when I say that I just don't care about how systems and processes work with your service desk and neither will *your* customers.

Always keep this sort of irrelevant information from your customers, EVEN IF IT IS TRUE.

I mention honesty throughout the book and believe it's essential for a great helpdesk, however you must become expert in judging the amount of information to divulge. You may be frustrated you can't get a customer what they need and what you've promised, however it is not benefitting anyone to share the intricate detail of why.

To the white goods company, and for your next habit trigger, the next time you're about to launch into a lengthy description about the limitations of your internal processes, how about this for an alternative approach?

"I'm really sorry Mr Copeman. It seems there has been an issue with this request and I'm going to personally talk to my manager later today to see how we can get this resolved for you asap.

I'll call you back on this number by the end of tomorrow."

Perfect.

To finish the story, I escalated this (as a point of principle more than anything else) and I did get the vouchers. Eventually.

Trigger > routine > reward

Internal process issues > Airing of dirty laundry > you can't blame me

Internal process issues > recognition there's an issue > finding an alternative solution for the customer

As a gesture (of good faith)

The last hollow phrase I'd like you to consider banning, appears in a continuation of the story from the previous topic. The letter I received with the vouchers, included two short paragraphs and one of them contained this phrase.

If your business uses this phrase in your written or verbal communications, you may as well be saying:

"We really didn't want to do this thing and we don't actually believe you, but feel we ought to because otherwise you're going to call up again and we just want the problem to go away."

I'd like to encourage you to stop using this phrase, written or verbal, because it immediately detracts from whatever you are offering. If you choose to use it, there's every chance it will leave a bitter taste with the customer.

"As a gesture, we've enclosed £50 of Amazon vouchers ..."

This phrase is quite often followed by ...

"however, in the future, we request ..." or *"but would request in the future you refrain from ..."* or *"and would now like to bring this matter to a close."*

Whilst you as a customer are happy to head down the high street with your new vouchers, you're still angry. You may have secured a small victory for yourself, but deep down, it's left a bad taste. You will still tell people of the bad experience, you may not return, and you will still be sceptical of that brand, all because of a thinly veiled apology.

If you're going to the effort of sending vouchers or offering some kind of compensation, you may as well make an apology - you have nothing to lose by making it, and in fact, everything to gain:

"We would like to apologise for the time you've spent on the phone to our team, while we resolved this internal issue.

It's a situation we've not seen before and we're going to put a solution in place to make this easier for customers in the future.

As a thank you for you bringing this to our attention, we'd like to enclose £50 of Amazon vouchers, which we hope you'll spend wisely.

If you have any problems with the fridge in the future. Please contact me directly."

Ahhhh ... I feel better already.

Trigger > routine > reward

We've messed up > "as a gesture" letter sent > that will get them off our back

We've messed up > genuine apology made > happier customer

Is there anything else I can help you with?

This is a common phrase, often planned into call centre scripts before a call comes to an end. Of course, there are some situations where it makes sense to use it. You've dealt with a request and the customer sounds like they have other things they need to resolve, or it just FEELS right to ask the question. Maybe you've even detected that they aren't in a rush to get off the phone (as opposed to the opposite).

There are however so many occasions where it's just not right to use it.

I heard it recently, having cancelled an account over the phone. The agent blindly followed the script...

"Is there anything else I can help you with today?"

I HAD JUST CANCELLED THE ACCOUNT. Of course there couldn't be!

I know I'm 47 and getting grumpier (just wait – it'll happen to you too), however the use of that autopilot, robotic response just makes me cross. I've cancelled the account because I was unhappy with the service, or no longer required it, and so wouldn't it make much more sense to say ...

"OK Mr Copeman, to confirm, I'm really sorry you've decided to cancel – that's all done for you now and you'll get an email confirmation shortly.

If you do change your mind in the next 48 hours, you can give me a call back before 6pm any day – my name is Stephen – I hope that's OK."

That would leave me with a warm feeling about the company, despite the fact I was leaving. It's also an indirect prompt to remind me if I've anything else I need to ask or query. It's inferred, without the need for the autopilot response.

I've also heard the phrase at the end of a call, where the situation hasn't even been resolved! Perhaps it was unresolvable, perhaps the agent just wasn't any good. Either way, I am about to end a phone call disappointed, having wasted 15 minutes of my life. To be asked if there's anything ELSE I need help with, clearly isn't the right thing to ask, as I've not been helped with anything up to this point anyhow!

Be more human

For me, this is the antithesis of 'human customer service'. Blindly making statements, irrespective of the situation, makes no sense.

If you're in charge of scripting and training, please stop asking your people to do this immediately!

If you're a helpdesk manager, encourage a common sense approach.

If you're an agent, I urge you to use common sense.

Your customers will thank you for it.

Trigger > routine > reward

Conversation about to end > standard phrase used > disjointed, robotic impression left

Conversation about to end > natural end to conversation > human sounding organisation

---

A final word on hollow phrases

I've scratched the surface here – there are so many other clichéd phrases which are used all around us every day. I hope you are now more aware of them and begin to identify and eradicate them as part of your working day.

Considering simple changes to each word and phrase you use with customers can make an enormous difference to how you are perceived as an individual *and* as a business.

Think about whether a phrase is used, just *because it's in the template*. Think about whether a phrase sounds automated. Then think about whether you should stop using it altogether.

Become more authentic and your helpdesk (skills) will move from good to great.

EMOTIONS

"The great gift of human beings
is that we have the power of empathy".

- Meryl Streep, actor

Introduction

Having seen the importance of developing the right communication habits, we now need to step up to the next layer of the ACETS pyramid and learn how to deal with Emotion.

As I'm sure you've already realised, being an agent is so much more than being a responder to tickets. Not only do you have to be an excellent communicator, but also a mediator and counsellor too. To truly understand a customer's reaction and how best deal with that reaction, you need to develop a few habits around understanding emotion. These habits should trigger regularly, particularly when difficult situations arise.

Develop and embed these habits and you'll find customer reactions start to make more sense to you and you'll feel more equipped to deal with seemingly irrational customers, because we've all had a few of those.

I want to encourage you, to open your mind as to what could be *really* going on around a customer when they write or call in. Sometimes the ticket or verbal request is the tip of the iceberg in terms of the issue they face, or the circumstances around them. Most customers will not communicate well. They will expect you to 'get' the situation in a heartbeat, often without fully explaining themselves. Becoming a helpdesk superhero, means understanding their state of mind, having empathy and developing rapport.

Each of these topics are all huge skills in their own right and aren't limited to your role as an agent – they are also skills you can practice in your personal life.

Let's get emotional.

Understanding empathy

As I'm sure you're starting to realise, and you won't need telling twice if you've been in your job for a while, a helpdesk agent has to be so much more than a product expert and enquiry handler. The job description may not reference it, but I suspect you're finding that you also need to be a mediator, a counsellor, a friend, a champion and a completer finisher.

> *The simplest customer service frustration question of all:*
> *"Why isn't this as important to you, as it is to me?"*
>
> Seth Godin

Rarely should you respond to an enquiry, without at least considering your customer's state of mind or situation they're in. Generally, verbal and written responses should be tailored, depending on your understanding of how they're behaving.

The alternative, is bland, vanilla responses, served up to anyone and everyone. Providing the right type of words in your responses back to customers each time will certainly make the job more interesting and make sure you keep customers for life.

> **Empathy,** *noun*
>
> *"the ability to understand and share the feelings of another."*

The words and phrases you choose to use will come about through your ability to be empathetic towards each customer. Once you get into the habit of thinking through the situation they *possibly* find themselves in and remembering the potential external factors which could be influencing them at that moment, you'll become a better agent.

Understanding or even making intelligent guesses at someone's drivers and figuring out why they are behaving as they are, means you'll be much better equipped to respond in the right way. You will naturally become more understanding, and so the right type of responses will just flow. When you don't think to put yourself into a customer's shoes, it can be easy to assume they are being unreasonable and so you respond accordingly.

The result of being empathetic

If you are empathetic to a situation, two things will happen:

- o A customer will know that you understand their situation and they will be calm and happy.
- o You will be more equipped to solve the problem, in the right way.

Happy and calm customers are what we all strive for. Having that wider understanding of their issues, either through assumption or questioning will help you to use the right words and get them onside.

Trigger > routine > reward

Difficult customer > react in a vanilla way > customer dealt with

Difficult customer > appreciate their situation through empathy and questioning > placated and happy customer

---

Be forensic

Empathy starts with having some appreciation of a customer's situation. That appreciation will almost certainly involve an extrapolation of the situation. In some cases, a customer will come on the line and explain their issue in great detail, outline the knock on effects and explain the consequences should things not be resolved. I think you'll appreciate, that's a rare occurrence.

More commonly, a customer will raise a ticket, for a seemingly innocuous problem.

Let's use an example of an old classic ...

The printer won't print

In many cases, if the printer didn't print, the requester would wait until someone else had fixed the problem. By then, the need to print may have vanished. It was a 'casual printing' situation.

However, in this scenario, a customer has just raised an urgent ticket and is showing signs of distress. Your understandable reaction might be to question what could be so urgent – surely, they don't need show signs of stress over printing something?

What if they were about to give the biggest speech of their life to an audience of 200 people and they'd left their original copy on the plane?

What if they were about to go on the biggest sales call of the quarter and had promised a hard copy of the presentation and proposal to their customer? The whole point of this meeting was to talk through it, sign the deal and free up cash, to fund the next three months of a failing business.

What if 10 new recruits had just started that morning and they need their contracts and induction packs that morning for signatures, enabling them to start their roles effectively?

What if you were about to deliver a paid training course and needed to print the feedback forms. Your monthly bonus is made up from the course evaluation scores?

Can you see how each of those situations (none of them too far-fetched I don't think?) have huge connotations for that requester hanging on the line to you right now. Being able to print, at that particular moment, is *the most important thing*. Those emotional customer moments should be your trigger for the empathy habit to kick in. Nothing else matters to your requester and your reading of that situation is critical, as it will influence your reaction and therefore resolution of the situation.

Now, this situation could present itself as a written ticket, stating simply that the printer won't print. There may not be any criticality attached to it. Another person might raise a ticket which could say urgent ... another might give the actual situation with specific timelines on it. Another person might call in and just rant! Everyone is different.

Your role as an agent in these situations is to have empathy. To create that state, often means asking questions, to find out what's really going on.

You might need to ask whether their request is urgent ... you might need the printer's location ID ... you might need to ask whether they're relying on it, and if so in what timeframe.

Asking the right questions will establish what the REAL issue is.

The printer not printing is a sub-issue. Worrying about getting fired by their CEO is the REAL issue.

As you see from this example, an enquiry is rarely a result of something isolated. There is normally a chain of events surrounding the ticket submission. A customer is looking to plan their day, their week, their month. Your response and your company's ability to deal with their query will often have a much bigger knock on effect and impact than you might at first realise.

Your actions will so often be part of a longer chain of events. It might be a small link perhaps, but an important one. Having empathy and an understanding of this chain will go a long way.

Questioning leads to better solutions

The other big benefit I've not already discussed, is that with that fuller understanding, you will be better equipped to deal with the actual issue. In the printer scenario, through empathy and questioning, you might have discovered that a customer has a speech to give. You now know it's an urgent requirement and can flag it accordingly.

Knowing the severity of the situation, thanks to your diligent questioning, means you can react to it proportionately.

You could send an engineer onsite within 30 mins, you could courier them a printout, you could dedicate a 2nd line support team member to fix the problem for the next two hours. All of these potential solutions might be costly to you as an organisation, but because you know the severity of the problem, the business case says that it makes sense to take drastic action and deploy the right resources.

On the flipside, if your empathy levels had been low, you could have taken that same drastic action, yet the customer's situation may not have been an emergency.

Calling in favours and deploying costly resources would have made bad business sense and the customer would have barely noticed the effort you'd gone to.

> **Trigger > routine > reward**
>
> *Situation to solve > jump to conclusion on issue > solve as normal*
>
> **Situation to solve > question and seek answers > best possible solution employed**

Create rapport

It's generally agreed that over 50% of building rapport is down to body language and so, when you're interacting with customers, you will always be at a 'rapport disadvantage' within a helpdesk environment.

Just because you aren't face to face, doesn't remove the need to create rapport. Instead, you need to work harder and be even more aware of the concept, to generate those bonds and generate them quickly.

I've had the pleasure of creating long standing relationships with customers I've never even spoken to, let alone met. I therefore know it's possible – it's just harder. Whether you're dealing with long term or 'single ticket' relationships, it's always good to strive for that immediate rapport. Here's my best advice on how to achieve it.

Be personal

Using a customer's name within sentences creates an immediate intimacy. In a social situation, if you've bothered to remember someone's name you've been recently introduced to, and use it in conversation with them, it initiates a bond. The same applies on a helpdesk.

Ensure you adopt the right tone. Use Mr or Mrs, or first name terms, depending on the situation. Older people tend to be more formal. If in doubt, follow their lead and let them correct you as appropriate.

I address this area in more detail in the 'Get personal' topic.

Be culturally appropriate

This is harder to prescribe – but be sensitive to someone's sex, race or religion where known. If someone with a French accent comes on the line and you are a French speaker, then offer to switch language.

Treat them with respect and where you have something in common – then use it to show you're on their wavelength.

Listen

Often rapport can be developed by saying nothing. Listening is so important. It shows you care. It shows you're looking to help if you're not interjecting. Give your customer space. Let them rant or explain their request and take a pause before responding.

Again, if you imagine a social situation, listening, nodding, indicating understanding as someone is talking helps to create a bond. Whilst there are no visual clues on the phone, your silence (or brief acknowledgments) show you're really listening.

Shared experiences

Depending on your topic of conversation, it may be hard to pick up on these areas, however through asking questions (a common theme throughout this book), you'll uncover different pieces of the customer's life and current situation.

Don't be afraid to be human. If you've bought a similar product, had a similar experience, are from the same town or also have a 5 year old daughter, then use that to your advantage. Of course, you need to get the balance right. Don't labour the point or take up more time than absolutely necessary. These precious moments can create a lasting impression on your customer (see 'Unconscious selling' in the next Layer) and make your company stand out. You will also have a more enjoyable conversation and find the ticket is much easier to deal with, when you've identified something in common.

Mirroring

Research says we tune in to and prefer people, who we perceive to be similar to ourselves. In a face to face situation, experts in rapport building will stand or sit in a similar way to the person they're talking to. Clearly this isn't possible with a helpdesk, however you can use similar techniques.

Whether written or verbal, you can mirror a customer's language by using formal or informal language and being to the point or being more verbose. If they like to talk technical, then you've carte blanche to wow them with your knowledge. On the flipside, less technically literate customers need to be treated accordingly. By listening carefully, you can come to these conclusions *before* using the wrong sort of language. Rapport will build quickly if the customer doesn't have to interrupt you, as you've already worked out their level of competence.

If you really want to master the subject, the FBI have published research in this area. They believe that mirroring speech patterns can also affect rapport. Matching the way your customer speaks can make a difference to a telephone relationship. Notice their pace, their timbre and their volume and temper your speech accordingly.

Trigger > routine > reward

Another ticket > respond as normal > another ticket answered quickly

Another ticket > be mindful of developing rapport > a happier customer and a more fulfilled agent

State of mind

When a customer behaves irrationally, it can be one of the hardest things to deal with as an agent. Whether they are angry, quirky or obnoxious, you will come across a complete cross section of the population in your role. Acknowledging each morning, that dealing with diversity is going to form a big part of your day is likely to be a big help.

Often, there's no explanation behind someone behaving in a 'different' way. Let's remember, we're dealing with the general public and they are a strange bunch, let me tell you.

Working for a SaaS business for 8 years, which reached the far corners of the globe, you inevitably hear from a small percentage of people who I would describe as 'definitely not normal'. From people WHO TYPE ONLY IN CAPS, to people who overreact to the most benign of comments. I've seen them all. It makes up the rich tapestry provided by the role though - and we should embrace it, because there's a learning opportunity at every turn.

It's not you

An immediate (and normally incorrect) reaction to these types of situations is to assume that *you've* done something specific to cause this customer's behaviour. This will not help in your reading of this situation - as the chances are, your actions won't have been the catalyst.

Assuming it's *not* you that has caused a situation, begin by reminding yourself that this customer may just be having a bad day. Whether it be work, career, family, finance, sometimes it helps to explain reactions, by reminding yourself that your customer could be having a really hard time and you're on the receiving end of their frustration.

Maybe they've just lost their job? Maybe they've just had some terrible health news? Maybe there's an issue with a loved one? You just don't know.

It happens to all of us. I'm sure you, dear reader, have had one or two moments of behaving irrationally or over reacting to a situation, because of your state of mind at that point in time. If you haven't, I'm impressed, but, secretly, I don't believe you!

The next time you have someone 'irrational' to deal with, trigger your 'state of mind' habit. Remind yourself that you don't know what's going on around them and in their life, and they may just be having a bad day.

Take a moment to be thankful that your day is clearly going much better than theirs – because you're in control of your emotions and not behaving irrationally. That's always been a help to me.

Trigger > routine > reward

Irrational customer > become angry back > it must be them not me

Irrational customer > interpret and appreciate their state of mind > a compassionate glow

Accept annoying bosses

Ever had a boss ask you to complete a task, you didn't agree with, or you were uncomfortable in carrying out?

You may have been asked to push harder for a sale, when deep down you know it's not the right thing to do. Maybe you've had to set 90 day payment terms or pressurised a supplier for a further discount, which you know will lose them money. Maybe you've had to make someone redundant or have been asked to behave in a way not consistent with your values. None of these things are easy.

I've seen people I've had relationships with suddenly change their minds or ask for something which was clearly outside of their value set. These sorts of interactions can be frustrating and difficult to explain, until you realise it could have been their boss pushing them to do it.

Pressure from above causes customers to act in strange ways. This is made harder when you already have a relationship with them and so know some of their personality traits. As an agent, you might be on the receiving end of that pressure. It might not be your customer's true voice. It might not be the actions *they* want to be taking.

When people are put under pressure to achieve a goal or complete a task, they often go about it the wrong way, because they're not comfortable doing it. Before you know it, they are making unnecessary demands, being aggressive with their questioning and putting you under more pressure than you would expect.

You need to bring your new found empathy habit into play again here. Whilst it may not be easy to spot that pressure from above is causing an issue, appreciating it is a *potential cause* of the behaviour, will help you begin to process, react and respond.

As I've discussed before, asking questions to establish the real drivers behind demands is so important. Use differing behaviour to trigger asking more questions. Play detective, get to understand what's really going on behind the scenes. If a customer knows you're trying to help, they are more likely to reveal what's really happening.

The next time *your* boss pressures you into behaving in a particular way, make a mental note about how you handle that pressure. Do you behave in a different way? Do you come across as more demanding? Remember that feeling – as it could explain the drivers behind the next customer you talk to.

> **Trigger > routine > reward**
>
> *Irrational behaviour > accept it > anything for an easy life*
>
> **Irrational behaviour > question whether a boss is at play > have a better and easier conversation**

Difficult questions

We've all been there. Whether you're highly trained and experienced or new in a job, someone will eventually ask you a question you don't know the answer to. It'll be something you've never been asked before. If it's not, this means you didn't solve this situation the last time - so shame on you!

'Something you've not been asked before' ... that's your trigger to get into the right mindset. It's an opportunity to learn, to find out the right answer from colleagues, from specialists or to work it out for yourself.

If your internal response to a question you don't know the answer to is that "I can learn to solve this ... I'm going to use this to benefit me as well as the customer", then congratulations, you've developed the correct mindset.

> "Develop a passion for learning.
> If you do, you will never cease to grow."
>
> Anthony J. D'Angelo, writer

Let's look at the customer perspective - they've asked a question to their interface into your business. Naturally they expect you to be able to answer anything and everything they throw at you. You are meant to be the expert.

"I don't know" ... "I'm not sure" ... "I don't think so" ... "hmmmm, maybe?" are all possible responses to a question you aren't able to answer.

If you choose to use one of those responses though, how will that customer be left feeling? Let down, annoyed, frustrated? They might put the phone down and try again, to see if another agent is more capable. They might receive your email response and can't continue with their day, as your answer impacted what they had planned.

The perfect answer

How about this as for an alternative approach?

"That's such a great question!

I've been doing this role for the last x years and no one has ever asked me that before!

I'm going to need to talk to some colleagues to get the right detail for you.

Can I put you on hold for 1 min / call you back? / I'll make sure I get you a response by close of play..."

This happened to me a lot in my Customer Thermometer days - normally on a live demo with a group of people within a large corporate organisation. They'd fire a highly detailed security related question at me, and I'd simply not know the answer.

I used a response similar to the one above every time. Prospects genuinely loved hearing it. It made them feel like they'd asked an intelligent question - that they were really engaged with the conversation.

Do you think anyone ever got upset that I couldn't give them an answer there and then? Of course not! I'd follow up in due course. I always took it as a positive buying signal, that someone had asked such a difficult question.

Customers are always delighted when an hour / day later you come back to them with a properly researched answer within the timescale you said. I feel this is a rarity in the helpdesk world - so take the opportunity to stand out and always follow through with your actions.

Your habit trigger here is your intended use of *"I don't know"*. This should now evoke the *"Great question!"* response.

With that positive mindset, you now have an opportunity to learn something new, make a customer feel special and delight them with your researched response.

> **Trigger > routine > reward**
>
> *Unsure of an answer > vague answer > not my problem any more*
>
> **Unsure of an answer > honest 'holding pattern' answer > happy customer within 24 hours**

Delivering bad news

Everyone must break bad news once in a while. Whether it's to an existing customer or prospect, no product or service can be everything to everyone. Compromise is inevitable, particularly when it comes to software.

"I need an engineer to be with me today – this is really urgent".

"I need to speak to a supervisor."

"I really need to set this account up, but I don't have a fixed address".

Process will often get in the way of delighting customers - and (sadly) quite rightly too. Any worthy business has to work by a set of rules, or it wouldn't grow and thrive. Having processes and rules means that in some situations, a customer won't be able to do what they want to do, despite your best efforts. This can mean that they wouldn't be a good customer for you anyhow.

You have rules for a reason - they work for your product or service… they make you profitable, they make you the success you are. Having different rules would change your margins, would add complexity to your product and potentially make your company less successful.

Don't fall into the trap of thinking that bending rules, accommodating all and constantly saying "yes" is a good thing for your business. It almost certainly isn't. Writing as someone who likes to please people a lot, this has been a hard lesson for me to learn. Understanding this rationale will help in your honest responses to customers who don't quite fit with your model. It really helped me.

Saying 'no' the right way

It's important to acknowledge that saying "no" is likely to be frustrating for a customer. Explaining why you do things in a certain way (succinctly) will go some way to helping disappointed customers to understand the reasons at least.

There is normally a positive way to respond to this type of situation. Your habit trigger for a *'can't'* type response should be, *'think alternative'*.

Example 1:

"No, the service can't do that I'm afraid. The good news is, that it can still get you close to what you need.

If you take a look at this help article [INSERT LINK] – you'll see that you'll be able achieve 80% of what you described to me. It's one of most popular features in fact."

Example 2:

"Yes, I understand why you would want that. The service can't do that at the moment, I'm afraid. It's actually a popular request and is on our roadmap right now.

I can't give you a definite timescale at the moment, but I can sign you up to our feature release bulletin if that would help?"

Example 3:

"No, we don't have that in stock at the moment – it's been a really popular item.

On a positive note, I can see we're getting a new shipment delivered very soon.

I can put this on back order for you, and it looks like you'll receive it within two weeks. Would that be helpful?"

Customers want solutions to their problems or desires. It's your job to solve their problem. Just because they've asked you for something specific, doesn't always mean that's what they *actually* want.

> Often, customers don't know what they need from you, they just *think* they know what they need.

When this concept was first pointed out to me, my confidence soared. Previously, I'd always responded to customer requests by taking them at face value. I didn't feel it was my place to impose my opinion on a customer (despite being an expert in my field).

When I realised, I had carte blanche to do the best I could for a customer and that it was actually the right approach, to provide your opinion, to say no, to suggest alternatives, it's quite exhilarating!

You're the expert. Ask more questions, get to the root of what they *really* need, and you'll start to have very different customer conversations.

You'll also keep customers for life.

Don't be vague

Half-hearted promises are the worst. Don't use them under any circumstances:

"I'll see what I can do".

"I'll talk to my manager".

"I don't think we can do that".

"I think we can do that".

Be honest! Don't be vague. Give a customer a straight answer. They'll thank you for that.

It means that they can then plan accordingly, they can move forward, make decisions and get things done. A half-hearted promise means that they can't do anything. You've given them false hope and they have to pause activities until they call back again, almost certainly, to hear bad news.

False promises are often just delaying bad news.

Make sure your team has somewhere to record these unfulfilled requests. Maybe the same request is being turned down every day? Maybe it's something the company should attempt to develop or resolve? Unless feedback is recorded, the product or service can't evolve.

> **Trigger > routine > reward**
>
> *Saying no > vague response or delivered without empathy > easy life*
>
> **Saying no > delivered with feeling and with options > customer is left feeling positive about the situation**

Dealing with angry customers

Dealing with angry or upset customers is part of agent life. Things will go wrong, customers will get upset – sometimes justifiably, sometimes less so. Remember, questioning and understanding the underlying issues can be really helpful in these situations.

If a delivery hasn't arrived, the *real* issue at stake is likely to be the knock on effect the delay has caused, rather than the delivery itself. If you'd ordered a bow tie, last minute, for a black tie event, and the package didn't arrive as promised, that's going to mean an unplanned journey to the shops. Pointing out to the customer they should have been more organised is our first lesson on how not to deal with angry customers 😊.

Calm down!

Here's a phrase not to use when dealing with an angry customer. Never tell a customer to calm down, as a result of their initial rant. The phrase itself tends to provoke an unwanted reaction, however there's another reason for removing it from your vocabulary.

When a customer has a complaint, always deal with that complaint directly. Never highjack the conversation by telling a customer what to do, as before you know it, you've created an argument and the customer will go from upset to furious.

The first habit I'd recommend is to always listen to the customer carefully before saying anything of real value. It pays to remember that you've two ears and one mouth in these situations. It could be they've rehearsed what they're going to say to you in advance, and so interjecting is going to disrupt their flow, making them even more frustrated.

Making an initial apology and focusing your efforts on solving the problem is what the customer is hoping for. Telling a customer how to act is never a good idea.

Reassurance is key

Throughout Helpdesk Habits, I talk about the need to communicate and ensure a customer knows that you understand their problem and secondly, are dealing with it effectively.

Reassuring a customer that you are there for them and are listening to their issues will mean you create trust, the first step to diffusing a difficult situation. You can only provide that reassurance by communicating effectively with the angry customer.

Here are some useful phrases.

"I'll let you explain the situation and then I'll find a solution for you."

"I can see why this is causing you a real issue – I'm going to do everything I can to get it resolved."

"My apologies. I can see why that's so frustrating. If need be, we can resend your order today, so you receive it before Tuesday. Please tell me exactly what happened, and I will get to work on fixing this."

"I'll make sure someone calls you before 2.00 to get things resolved. Please do not worry."

Empathy and reassurance go hand in hand as you can see. Demonstrating to a customer that you 'get it' will go a long way to calming a customer down and showing them that you are the right person to get things resolved for them.

Use the facts

If the customer's anger is making the call difficult to deal with, aim to keep things factual. Simply outlining the situation encourages them to focus on their communication, shows them you're listening and making progress and so makes it harder for them to maintain an aggressive tone.

It's also useful to give the customer an idea of how you're going to fix the issue. Whilst *you* may be confident in your abilities to get things done, *they* don't know anything about you or the process you are following.

Tread the fine line between communicating and saying more than you need to. Experience will tell you when to stop.

Be positive

Assuming the customer's anger towards an issue is justified, it's now time for you to offer a solution. Never say 'no' or be negative if you can help it. Instead, focus on the positive things that you can offer or do for them to resolve their problem.

Of course, sometimes damage is irreparable and being positive is hard. Be creative – find a way to offer a solution and make that customer at least appreciate you've tried to help. In other situations, you won't be able to offer a solution there and then and will need to get back to them. Be precise – explain what's going to happen before you end a conversation and thank them for being patient.

"I've involved my supervisor, Kelly Jones, and she will be calling you back before 2.00 today."

"I know we can't get you exactly what you need, but will this alternative help you out of this situation?"

> Do try not to take matters personally.
>
> The angry customer is angry with your company or the situation, as opposed to *your* actions.

Think of yourself as the lucky one – you've an opportunity to shine and make things right.

Remind yourself of the power of the Service Recovery Paradox.

Trigger > routine > reward

Angry customer > heart sinks, fight fire with fire > don't have to deal with them again

Angry customer > Service recovery paradox reminder > opportunity to shine and be remembered

TACTICS

"Practice does not make perfect.
Only perfect practice makes perfect."

- Vince Lombardi, American Football legend

Introduction

Having dealt with some of the harder to master human skills needed to be a great customer service agent, it's now time to climb the ACETS pyramid once again and get tactical.

The top two layers are all about tactics, some more advanced than others. They are a collection of ideas I've used and discovered over many years of dealing with customers at all levels. Some will be obvious to you, some less so. The reason I've collated them in this book, is because each one of them can be developed into a habit.

As you keep layering on habit after habit, you'll get better and better at dealing with customers. As these habits spread across your team, you'll soon be seen as a set of superheroes and will be helping your business to stand out from the crowd.

I do understand that resources around you are finite. You are unlikely as an agent to be able to pick and choose how you spend your time or how you're measured. Your company will have queuing systems, priorities, processes and ways of working and so at first glance, some of these habits may be harder to embed than others.

Key to success with this Layer, is being inspired and taking these ideas to the powers that be. Explain that you've started to develop certain habits and you'd like them to develop across your team. I hope you're in a business where you feel you're able to do that.

You're about to learn all about encouraging complaints, harvesting testimonials, leaving tickets overnight, documenting, selling without realising and much more. It's a smorgasbord of habits which when embedded, will get you close to becoming that helpdesk superhero.

Understand urgency

When a customer contacts your helpdesk, it means they are working with your product or service *right now*. They likely have a small window of time scheduled to evaluate your software, use your product or complete a task for a manager, colleague or customer.

Put yourself in their shoes for a moment.

When they run up against an issue, they are writing or calling in as a last resort. They will have no desire to involve another human if they can possibly help it. They know that will involve waiting, not receiving an immediate response and possibly getting bad news back too.

Most customers will try everything in their power to solve their own problem - using your knowledgebase, FAQ, their own brain or possibly even turning it on and off ...

Raising a ticket is not something anyone does for fun. It's done as a last resort. Typically, the need to contact a helpdesk will disrupt someone's day and mean that they can't get to do what they'd planned to do.

It's sometimes easy to forget the disruption, frustration and knock on effect, that raising a ticket can cause.

Timely responses

Because your customer has had their day disrupted, speed of response is crucial to keeping that customer on side.

To enable that customer's day to continue smoothly, in a perfect world, they would receive an immediate response from you. The net result would mean no disruption to their plans. *If* your helpdesk is set up to triage and respond to simple requests within minutes, you *will* look like superheroes, because of the lack of impact on that customer's day.

Basecamp, the renowned project management software business, publishes its average response time. At the time of writing, it's 9 minutes. Which is impressive.

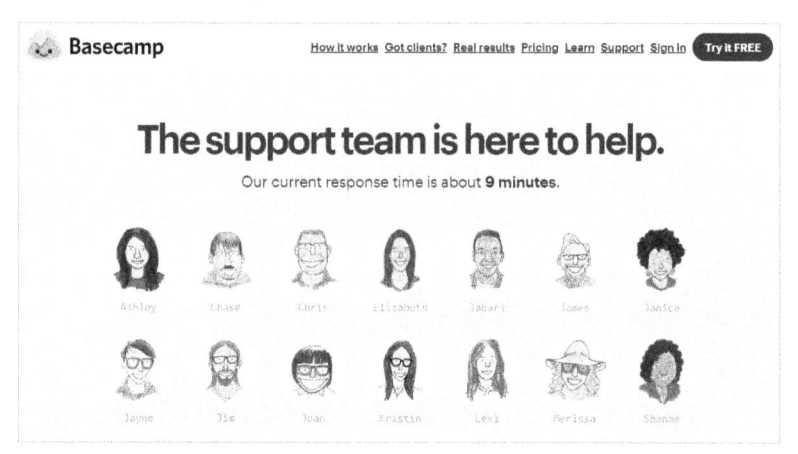

Basecamp's support page

Many other helpdesks publish wait times too, sometimes in the ticket acknowledgement email. Sadly, it's not uncommon to see several days as a predicted response time. For me, that's just not good enough. If you think back to what I've already mentioned around impact - you can see that's seriously disruptive.

I've seen with my own eyes, the effect a fast response ticket turnaround can have on a customer. You'll find customers (and prospects) are amazed if they receive a response within a few minutes. They are grateful too. Why? Because you've saved their day from disruption and they can continue with their plans.

I had customers complementing Customer Thermometer on a response received, within a *working day*. They've expressed genuine surprise that their request hadn't gone into a black hole and that they've got something useful and workable back within a day, meaning they can forge ahead with their plans.

Triage works

Sadly, (yet happily for you), the 'time to respond' bar is generally set low. The perception of customer service across most sectors, is that response times are long, and for larger companies, that they may not even get a response. Your business has a chance to shine, if it can regularly respond quickly.

Key to success for me, is triaging your queue. *Maybe* it makes sense to treat presales enquiries with greater urgency? Perhaps a customer needs a single, simple response to buy. They are poised with their credit card and need one question answered. Could that ticket and therefore sale be closed within 5 minutes?

Some would say it's wrong to give pre-sales priority over existing customers. It depends on your business. If you're not disrupting a customer's day, by responding to them within an hour, then you should absolutely focus on closing presales first.

> *"Move fast. Speed is one of the main advantages over large competitors."*
>
> **Sam Altman, Successful angel investor**

If you can respond to 90% of customers with simple to answer requests, within an hour, why wouldn't you? More difficult requests which take time to research should perhaps be treated differently. Communicate in a timely way though. Set expectations with a customer that there will be a delay in response. Give them a timescale and deal with their request as appropriate. Few people will not be satisfied when being dealt with in that way.

For the wider team

I appreciate much of what's discussed in this topic may be out of your direct control. If you can't make these changes, show this page to someone who can!

> ### Trigger > routine > reward
>
> *Follow up needed > take tickets in order > first in, first out is fair*
>
> **Follow up needed > triage to delight the majority with rapid responses > raised satisfaction and increased sales**

Keep your promises

As a consumer dealing with any type of helpdesk, there is nothing more frustrating than having to chase for an answer or action.

When a promise has been made for a call back or a written response and it doesn't arrive, it creates the worst impression. You possibly have experience of predicting a broken promise will happen, however you are a positive person and like to give the agent the benefit of the doubt. You might even use phrases like:

"So, you're definitely going to be sending this confirmation by 2.00?"

To ensure the lines of communication are clear.

Then, nothing.

When dealing with larger organisations, it's all too easy to assume that once communication is severed, nothing further will happen until you call and pressurise.

On the flipside, we will all be delighted with a customer service experience when a helpdesk has done what they said they were going to do. It's quite a shocking thing to write really. Why would we be delighted about something which should happen naturally? Because, it's unusual.

> When a helpdesk gets its processes right and an agent does what they say they are going to do, it's natural to feel pleasantly surprised.

The good news is that it's so easy to stand out. We can use this customer service 'rarity' to our advantage, by always following through, and by keeping our promises to customers.

Be on time

Timeliness must apply to the commitments you make during the process of solving an issue. If you promise to get back to a customer with an answer to a question you need to research, always commit to a timescale.

Always under promise and over deliver.

Timeliness isn't about immediate responses. Customers understand that's not always possible, and normally don't need that speed of response. They want to know their request is being dealt with and they want to understand *when* they are likely to receive an answer, in order to plan their day and get things done.

"I hope that's answered your first two questions and will help you move forward.

The third question is trickier! I'm going to need to check with a colleague, as I want to make sure my answer is accurate. Please bear with me until 2.00 today and I'll update you then.

If you do need an answer sooner, let me know asap."

Any customer would be delighted to receive such a helpful response. Make sure you beat that 2.00 deadline though, or your good work and words will be undone.

Letting a customer know *when* they'll get an answer means they can then plan ahead. It's so easy to forget that the answer they require is rarely isolated. It's likely that the answer you're promising, will form a link in a much bigger chain of events.

When making a promise of a response to a customer, get into the habit of setting a reminder or alert. It's all too easy to get distracted by other issues. Post-it notes aren't the answer to your reminder system either – put something robust in place, which works for you and your business.

This type of practice will set you apart as a helpdesk agent and your actions will go some way to setting your company apart too.

Trigger > routine > reward

Promise made > distracted by activities > they'll get in touch – it's not my problem any more

Promise made > reminder set, action taken, customer updated > remarkable customer service

---

Unconscious selling

As a point of clarification, this topic is nothing to do with outbound telesales. That's not a subject I'm ever likely to write about. I think we'll park that back in the 90's perhaps? For me, it's just not a component of a sales strategy today.

Selling. This scary-to-many word has so many different connotations and means many things to different people. If you're someone who thinks "selling" is a 'dirty' word – then I'd like to explain to you why I think you're wrong.

"I'm not a sales person... I can't do sales."

People do tend to categorise themselves into those that can sell (or at least claim they can) and those that can't (or at least claim they can't). Which side of the fence do you sit?

Their opinions are normally based on the stereotypical double glazing salesperson knocking on your front door, the car salesman, or the market trader.

They are described as stereotypical roles for a reason – they are for hard core sales people only, using a specific set of techniques. There are many other methods of selling.

Consider this:

> **People can't be sold to,
> however you can help people to buy.**

It's a belief I've held for many years and have practiced a lot. If you're in the mindset that you're not a 'salesperson', these next few paragraphs may help you to see the light.

As you are part of a helpdesk team, appreciating and recognising explicitly that a big part of your responsibility is selling (often in an indirect way) will really help you master your role.

Regardless of the type of organisation you work for, or its market vertical, when a customer or prospect contacts your organisation and you respond, for that moment, you *are* the face of that company. Product, history, brand, perception and pricing become irrelevant. That contact's opinion of your entire company will be influenced by your actions.

Scary thought isn't it?

Small interactions, big impacts

Let's look at an example of this concept from outside of the helpdesk world. I'll then relate it back.

You've just returned from a vacation and are telling a friend all about your travels. The flights were on time, the booking experience was simple, the price was right, and you were able to travel to and from a local airport.

Scenario 1:

Throughout the outbound flight, the cabin crew were efficient, they left you an extra bottle of wine, enjoyed a joke and a smile and spent 30 seconds chatting to you about your children and something you had in common. At the end of the flight, they smiled, said goodbye and wished you a great holiday.

Your story to your friend might start something like this:

> "AcmeAir, [insert any airline here] – oh they're brilliant – I'd always travel with them".

Scenario 2 (the previous conditions around price, booking etc are identical to #1):

Throughout the outbound flight, the cabin crew were obnoxious, barely spoke to you, had little eye contact with you and didn't remember to get the glass of water you asked for shortly before landing. On disembarking, you overheard them chatting in the galley about their weekend and how tired they were.

Your story then might start something like this:

> "AcmeAir, [insert any airline here] – oh we had a terrible flight with them – I'd always avoid them if I can"

Can you relate to these two scenarios? Your *entire* opinion of an airline, is influenced by a handful of small interactions, lasting in total, probably only a minute or two.

Can you see how *you* could have that same influence over a customer? A single phone call or an email thread, can change the perception of someone's opinion of your entire company.

That, is selling.

It may not be selling in the traditional sense. You're not asking someone to part with their money, you're not trying to upgrade them, but you are laying the foundations for a continued relationship, or their next purchase from you. You are effectively helping people to buy (in the future).

> *"Selling is helping people to do what they're already inclined to do."*
>
> **Daniel Pink, Author**

So, even if you've labelled yourself as someone who can't sell, you might want to think again. Maybe you've been selling indirectly for years without realising?

Selling doesn't have to be a dirty word. It can be quite the opposite when done correctly. Talk with your team. Make them appreciate the importance of 'unconscious selling'.

Take that realisation a step further and develop new habits for spotting opportunity and feedback.

Tiny amounts of effort can reap huge dividend.

> **Trigger > routine > reward**
>
> *Customer conversations > follow the manual > just doing my job*
>
> **Customer conversations > appreciate you're currently the face of the company > being proud to make a difference**

Encouraging complaints

At first glance, you might find this a strange topic title. Why on earth would you want to *encourage* customers to complain? Surely a complaint is the last thing you want to hear?

Actually, no.

Studies have shown that vast the majority of unhappy customers don't bother complaining, they simply stop doing business with you, without warning.

This is tricky to reconcile, as if you aren't receiving complaints, it can seem that all is well with the world and all customers are happy. Why on earth would you meddle?

The reason for digging a little deeper here, is that receiving *no* complaints means something's not right. It's likely you've no complaints because customers find complaining a stressful experience. Even if your business makes it easy for customers to complain, the vast majority never will, as it's *perceived* as too much effort.

People tend to shy away from difficult conversations and so why would you give up your time to provide constructive feedback if you were going to leave anyway? Why not just leave? It's not as if the company's going to do anything with my complaint anyway – or will they?

> *"We all need people who will give us feedback. That's how we improve."*
>
> Bill Gates, Philanthropist

It turns out that requesting feedback and therefore opening yourself up to complaints is one of the best ways to retain customers.

There's possibly another book in me around the topic of asking for feedback, but I shall save that for another year. This book is all about the habits you as an agent must develop to become a superhero. So, assuming your organisation is open to feedback, what can you do, as an individual, to impact positively in this area?

Your attitude to complaints

It's natural to become defensive when a customer has a complaint. The oldest structure within your brain is called the 'reptilian' brain, as it is thought we've inherited it from our prehistoric ancestors. It is programmed to respond to threat using one of four mechanisms: appease, freeze, flight or fight. It's not uncommon to respond to a complaint (a threat) with fight. We do that, because it's a natural response and you are loyal to your organisation and so you understandably want to defend it.

"It's not our fault the courier was late."

"Our network provider had an outage – it wasn't under our control."

The next time you receive a complaint as a front line agent, use your habit trigger to view the story that's about to be related as a *'gift'*, rather than a threat. That's right, feedback is a gift, which is the view of so many, including the likes of Warren Buffet.

Remember, it's unlikely the complaint is going to be about you – it will be about your organisation and so there's no need to take it personally. You should avoid the natural tendency to defend what's happened. Instead, listen intently. Record the complaint, apologise as appropriate and make sure that it's then sent to the relevant team for action and analysis.

Impromptu feedback

I'd encourage you as an agent or helpdesk manager to ensure you've a robust feedback system in place, which makes it easy for customers to complain and praise, yet without intruding. Even if you don't have the remit to make that happen, there should be enough evidence in this topic for you to make a persuasive argument to your team.

Regardless of a wider programme, agents can really make a difference on the front line, as feedback will be provided in a variety of ways throughout the day. Whether written or verbal, whether praise or complaint, whether about process or features, you have a duty to make sure valuable feedback is recorded in the right way.

Sometimes the feedback will be proactive or woven within a customer response. A great habit to develop is the ability to identify feedback – isolate it from the surrounding words and provide it to those that can benefit from it.

Occasionally, the opportunity presents itself to get proactive and ask a customer for feedback as a natural part of the conversation.

"I'm really glad you found that piece of advice helpful – do you think it's the sort of thing we should be publishing regularly on our website?"

"I know we let you down here – what would you have liked to have seen happen instead?"

Get into the habit, as part of your human customer service ethos, of soliciting for feedback as part of a natural conversation. You'll be amazed at what you learn.

Trigger > routine > reward

Customer complaint > switch to defensive mode > we showed them it wasn't our fault!

Customer complaint > listen hard > a complaint is a gift - make change with your learnings

Harvest testimonials

I spoke to and swapped emails with customers and prospects dozens of times a day during my time at Customer Thermometer. As a result, I had a rich seam of potential customer quotes extolling the virtues of our service, landing regularly in my mailbox. It was nothing short of a goldmine of marketing nuggets.

Every time a compliment came in, I simply wrote back to the customer and asked them if they were happy for us to use that quotation on our happy customers page (which you can find on the Customer Thermometer website). It was rare they said no. I went a step further with some customers and asked for a fuller interview via video / audio / text. We published those regularly too.

Over the years we had an ongoing programme to renew and add to that page. My aim was to make the page overwhelming, so that when prospects did look for that all important social proof about our software, they were met with a wall of positivity, making the service irresistible to sign up to.

The reverse situation is common.

I was with a consulting client recently. He kept telling me amazing customer stories. He could pull stories of success and quotations from the depths of his brain for hours, detailing just how brilliant his service had been for his customers over the years.

His team didn't know about these stories. I know that, because I interviewed them. They weren't displayed on the website and they weren't being used in marketing materials. Instead, the marketing gems were buried away in 10 years of emails and in the far reaches of the founder's brain. He realised his mistake quickly and we've since rectified things!

How can you help?

Where does your helpdesk role fit in here? Do you have a process for passing on positive quotations to your team? Do you ever ask for customer testimonials? Is there a rich seam of marketing and sales materials buried away in thousands of tickets over the years?

Unless you get into the habit of spotting these types of comments, they can easily pass you by.

It's also easy to get blasé about positive comments coming through to you and assume everyone knows your business is amazing. I promise you, they really don't unless you tell them!

This sort of case study feedback is one of the greatest assets any company can own and it's often all around us. Make sure you harness it and contribute to the sales effort indirectly.

Trigger > routine > reward

Happy customer writes with comment > ticket closed > Yay – ticket closed!

Happy customer writes with comment > comment utilised > a brand new testimonial is born

---

Check before sending

The joy of responding to a ticket ... completing what you think to be a great response, particularly if it's around a sticky subject, or to a difficult customer, gives you a great feeling. There's almost a feeling of relief to have got to an answer or resolution and all you have to do now is press send and you can move on. Hopefully to something more straight forward.

Don't rush to get it off your plate.

Don't hit send. Yet.

Like all good pieces of writing, you need to let it sit. You need to make sure your response is the best it possibly can be.

How many times have you completed a ticket, rushed it back to the customer, only to be bitten again shortly afterwards and that sinking feeling comes back? If you have similar habits to an old mindset *of mine*, of trying to get things out the door quickly, then I suspect it's happened a lot.

Do you recognise the feeling of hitting a send button with one eye almost closed, slightly turned away from your screen, with a feeling of '*I'm sure it'll be fine ...*' running around in your mind?

That's your habit trigger. When you feel those kinds of emotions or recognise that send button click with an almost embarrassed feeling, it's time to stop, reflect and change that habit!

Recognise the signs

The reason for that semi-embarrassed feeling is that you know the customer is going to come back to you quickly ... they aren't going to be satisfied with your answer for any number of reasons.

Perhaps they won't understand how to complete something you've prescribed?

Perhaps they won't accept or even believe your answer?

Perhaps you know that they won't like the bad news you're giving them?

Perhaps you know you're trying to qualify in, a prospect who wouldn't be a good fit for your business?

Perhaps you're not even answering their question properly, or only a proportion of it?

Subconsciously, you know one or some of these things are true when you hit the send button, but secretly, you're hoping to get away with it.

We've all had that feeling. 99 times out of 100 you won't get away with it either, and rather than writing that one awesome response and the ticket being closed and the customer being content with the response, you end up spending half the week responding to the thread or taking their calls.

Clearly that's not good use of time. Perhaps more importantly, that's not great for your mental state either!

So, let's figure out how to avoid this type of scenario happening.

Before you hit that send button, there's a mental check list to run through. Some of these items can be skipped if it's a benign response. All of them need to be ticked if you're dealing with a tricky, nagging ticket or a difficult customer.

Check for suitable language

When you review your response, think about the customer you're writing to (if you know them personally). If you don't know them and you can only react to the words on the ticket, match your language to theirs. If they're informal, you should go in that direction too.

If they sign off as Mr Smith, address them as Mr Smith. Details like that really matter to many people. The little things will always get noticed and remembered - one of the key tenants of this book. Multiple, small actions compound to create something much bigger.

Check for word count

I've mentioned previously, that I was taught to reread an email and take out as many words as I could. That's really stuck with me. So often when you create an initial draft of a response, you use more words than necessary.

Go through every line and look to remove additional words or rewrite sentences with fewer words.

Why? Because less is more.

The fewer words in the response, the clearer it will be and the more likely it will be understood.

Fewer words *shouldn't* mean less 'warm in tone', however. Strike a balance.

Make sure it's personal

Is your sign off and/or signature correct? Add a PS with something quirky or personal, only if you think it's appropriate.

Customers will always love the personal approach. Remember your 'Human customer service' ethos.

Have you answered the question(s)?

Customers often ask multiple questions on a single thread. Have you answered them all or just the one or two that you know the answer to? Are you secretly hoping they won't notice the one you've not answered? Bad news. They will! You can rest assured it's probably the most important one to them too.

And finally

As you get more practiced at responding to tickets and harnessing some of the tactics in this book, the need to check a response will become less over time, as you'll be more familiar with the details you should be looking for, as you write them.

Until that point, check, check, check and avoid that one eyed, looking slightly away send button click ...

Aim to feel proud of your responses every time.

Trigger > routine > reward

Ticket completed > hit send > look at my speed of response!

Ticket completed > thorough response check > ticket closed

Let it sit

Once you've completed a ticket, it's not always possible to leave a response in your drafts for hours or overnight, but for those difficult responses, it can be of real benefit.

If the situation allows for it, let it sit. You'll see your response in a very different way the following day and your task of editing will become more obvious.

Letting it sit is a particularly good idea if you're dealing with an angry customer. If you've been sent an unjustified or semi-abusive email, it may be your reaction to fight fire with fire. This is never a good idea! Always be professional. Letting a response sit overnight will always ensure you treat a difficult situation with a cool head.

Can someone else help?

If you are dealing with a really 'thorny' issue or tricky customer and you've written your best possible response, ask whether it would make sense for a colleague read it over with an open mind. Ask them to wear the customer's shoes for a moment. Describe the situation. Ask them to be honest and edit the response as required. Two brains are better than one.

I do this a lot both inside and outside of the customer service domain, particularly for high value or difficult customers. It's amazing how another pair of eyes (ideally linked to that second brain I've mentioned) can make a difference and challenge what you've written.

Always keep an open mind to their feedback. You'll enjoy a different perspective – not just for the current ticket, but for the way you respond to tickets in the future.

Be practical

With target response times to hit and customers to serve, I'm the first to be pragmatic. Letting responses sit, impacts metrics and isn't always practical.

That said, ask yourself the price paid for rushed, inaccurate responses versus, letting a customer wait a few hours for the *right* response.

Where time is pressing, and you can't afford to let a response sit, do the next best thing and refer to the previous, "Check before sending" topic as a fall back.

Trigger > routine > reward

Controversial or difficult response > just get it sent > the customer deserved it!

Controversial or difficult response > take a pause where practical > no regrets on sending

---

Always be documenting

So far, everything in Helpdesk Habits has been focused around helping customers, which is absolutely correct. In the final two topics of this Tactics layer, I want to talk about the importance of your helpdesk team. Forming habits for the benefit of your colleagues, helpdesk team and business is vital to providing a rounded customer experience.

> Say 'aye!' if *you* like to
> document processes, activities or issues.

Silence.

Yes, I thought so. It's not something which is going to get anyone excited, however I'm going to attempt to do that during this topic.

My personal experience as an agent for Customer Thermometer really opened my eyes to the power of writing up the things that matter. When you're a one or two person business, it's hard to imagine having a wider team, when you can shout across a room and so it's easy to get into the habit of recording conversations on Post-it notes or filing them away in the back of your brain. This type of approach to customer documentation will eventually cost your business thousands of hours each year. It will also impact customer relationships.

Ticketing system

Whether you're working on the phone or via email, you will have a ticketing system in place. The system may be loved or loathed, but it's the system and needs to be used.

I'm going to assume that you're diligent at updating tickets. If you're not, then you'll be getting a call from your boss very soon I'm sure!

I want to encourage the habit of adding more than just ticket information where practical. You probably have an internal notes area for tickets and customers. When additional information about that customer is going to help the next agent, who might need to deal with them or the ticket, then add it.

"David can get quite angry – he's had a number of service failures with us in the past and we need to go out of our way to answer promptly and accurately over the coming months."

Yes, there may be all kinds of flags and analytics which are designed to flag at risk customers, but human customer service applies internally too. It's incredibly helpful to the team to know about David's past in a single clearly written note. Agents then don't have to comb through reams of notes or tickets to make that connection. They can immediately deal with David in the most appropriate way.

Taking time out to update colleagues on a customer persona can save customer relationships and make your helpdesk team look like superheroes, because they react to individual customer situations.

Knowledgebase & FAQ

I struggle to think of a more valuable tool for a helpdesk team. If your company doesn't have a well-designed, accurate and uptodate knowledgebase for your customers to self-serve, then put this book down immediately and make it happen!

As I've already written, Knowledgebases save hours for both customers and agents, as a common set of information can be shared easily. Lengthy ticket replies can be replaced, and, in many cases, tickets won't be raised, as customers can self-serve.

Knowledgebases are their own worst enemy, as normally the day after they are launched, they are then left to languish. They are rarely updated as there is no process or owner and so a brilliant resource quickly becomes outdated, which is often worse than not having one at all, as you are providing incorrect information!

If you're looking for inspiration, [Search: *customer thermometer help*], for a brilliant example of a knowledgebase, which really is kept uptodate.

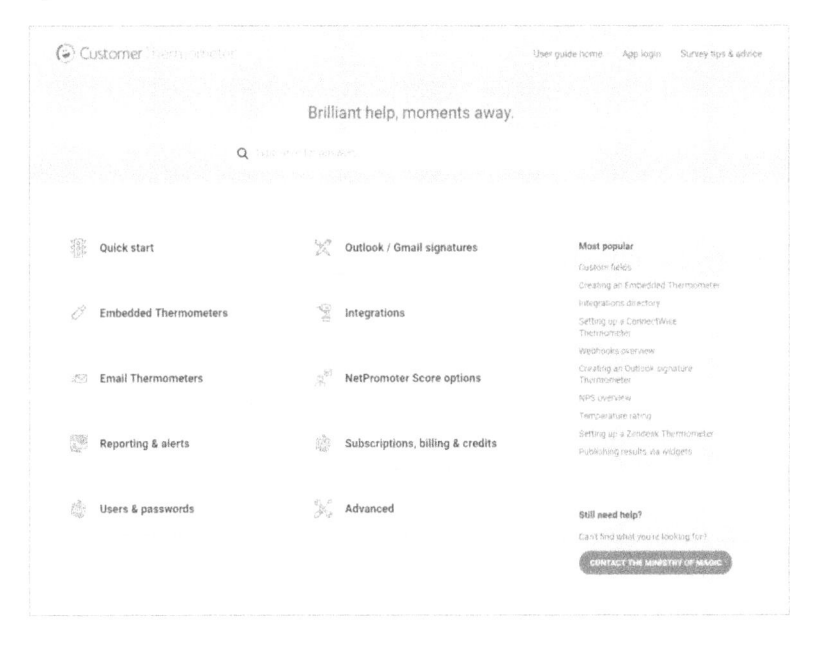

Customer Thermometer's knowledgebase

You and your helpdesk colleagues have a big part to play here. Few people are more qualified to own and update this resource. You know the most common questions. You know the best way answers should be provided. You know the hot topics.

Develop a team habit today to review your knowledgebase regularly. Common replies should be logged and added to the knowledgebase. When you link to a knowledgebase page, review it first – don't just send it blindly. Check, to the best of your knowledge, that it's uptodate and accurate.

If everyone gets into the habit of being diligent with this precious resource, it will thrive.

Make a start today!

> **Trigger > routine > reward**
>
> *Opportunity to contribute > not really my job > tea break*
>
> **Opportunity to contribute > update resources > team player**

Sharing is caring

Following on from the previous topic, so much of my inspiration at Customer Thermometer came from other members of the team. We were a remote organisation and so overhearing conversations and shouting across a room was never an option.

Because we worked remotely, it meant we had to actively share experiences, anecdotes and learning. Without this focus on sharing, it was never going to happen naturally.

What to share?

Your helpdesk will have its own quirks and depending on whether you've 100 customers of 100,000, the experience will be very different.

Customer updates are always important. Knowing some of the nuances which would never appear on a ticket will always be helpful. Update teams on delicate negotiations or particularly emotional or irrational contacts. Share recent agent experiences about what to say and what not to say.

> There's no single correct solution to knowledge sharing, but creating routine and habits around sharing is always beneficial.

As your helpdesk evolves and gets more sophisticated, the tools you're using will need to keep up. If you don't discuss as a team, where tools need changing, updating or configuring, then the powers that be can never make them right. Make a point of discussing where tools are hindering productivity and make proactive suggestions for changes.

Your knowledgebase(s) and FAQ should be an ongoing topic of discussion. Encourage updates and additions regularly from your frontline team. No one else in your organisation is better equipped to bring this tool alive.

Consider sharing development needs and get to understand those in your team who are becoming specialist in certain areas. No one person can be expert in all aspects of your helpdesk – encourage the cross-pollination of skills amongst teams to upskill those who need it. Knowing 'go to' people for certain disciplines is really helpful.

Finally, the rest of the business needs to know what your helpdesk team is doing. Take the opportunity to share news with other departments. Let them know about the testimonials programme you're running. Let them know about the case studies you've uncovered. Let them know about the product feedback you're documenting every day.

They'll be glad to hear from you 😄.

How to share?

Some people are natural communicators. They will write copious blog posts and internal notes and think nothing of shouting from the rooftops about a recent experience. This is great, however encouraging those that are more reluctant to communicate is key to ensuring a balance of information flows.

If I ask my son how his day has been, I'll get a full list of activities, emotions, triumphs and disappointments.

The same question to my daughter will reveal,

"Good."

I'll of course continue to question her and will eventually hear about the flapjacks she's baked and the Latin teacher exploding, due to the sniggering at the back of the class.

I then have a full, unbiased picture of both of their days.

The same scenario may apply within your team. It's therefore important to allow everyone to have a forum and to share what they know to get the right balance.

Create an agenda item for a Monday morning team meeting entitled 'show and tell'. Ask all team members to prepare a one minute anecdote each week. Make sure those anecdotes are then recorded against tickets, within internal or external knowledgebases or are plastered on posters on walls if it's worthy.

For remote workers, encourage 'Slack type' equivalent conversations. Ensuring there's a specific time of the week or day for this to happen means more reluctant team members have to contribute. Ad hoc sharing means the verbose ones will hog the limelight (*looks away).

> **Trigger > routine > reward**
>
> *Monday morning > carry on in isolation > get more tickets answered*
>
> **Monday morning > listen and learn from others' experiences > true collaboration and teamwork**

Sign off sincerely

I don't know how much thought has gone into your team's sign offs or signatures? Maybe it's something that has never been discussed or maybe you've a signature file which is updated on a weekly basis? Most ticket signatures I see, have had little thought sadly, which makes it another chance for you to shine.

A ticket sign-off should be a marketer's dream. It's an opportunity to put a message, a brand and a personality in front of your customers multiple times each day, for free! You have a captive audience as they are actively looking for a response from you.

Take an action right now to look at your signature file. What does it say about you and your company? Is it consistent across your colleagues? Has it been updated this year?!

> *"People buy personalities and ideas much more quickly than they buy merchandise"*
>
> **Napoleon Hill, author**

Make it personal. Ensure your name is used in the sign-off – not *'From the helpdesk team'*. Adding a photo is becoming more common, although I saw a response recently from a company, with a photo in the signature and no name – which actually looked a bit sinister. They'll be getting a copy of the book in the post 😊.

I think a photo is a great thing (providing it's a decent, appropriate shot) – it's personal and you certainly can't be accused of being faceless.

Make the rest of your signature consistent with your colleagues. Make it designed, on brand – make sure it contains your logo, a central phone number and email address, so that customers can access contact information easily, by recalling the last email.

My other recommendation would be to add a simple request for 1-click feedback ...

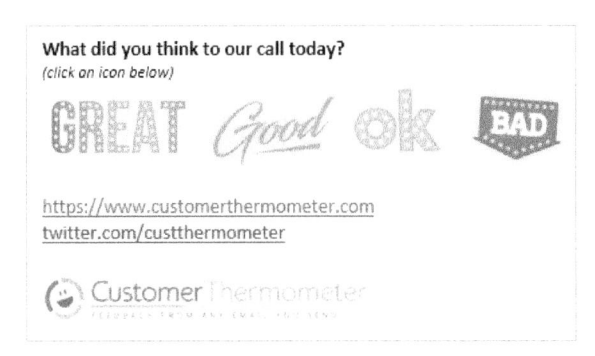

I'm of course biased, however definitely check out Customer Thermometer's service, which integrates with all the major ticketing systems. This is a great personal touch, as it allows customers to rate you *and* provide feedback, within a ticket (as opposed to a request in a separate email). It also doesn't impact on a customer's time, as the transaction can be completed in seconds.

My final suggestion is so rarely implemented, yet could have a massive impact on your business. It's a decision more for your wider team than for you as an individual. If you mention it though, you'll be awarded gold stars ...

> Have you considered using simple
> banner adverts in your signature?

They can be highly targeted, based on your queue or team and can sow seeds with ticket requesters who are already either customers or prospects. As they're interacting with your helpdesk already, it's a natural next step to promote something of interest, and allow them to click through for more information.

Talk to your marketing team – ask them if they'd be interested in getting in front of 100, 1000, 10,000? contacts per day.

For free.

I suspect they will be 😌.

Trigger > routine > reward

Templated response required > no personalisation > easy life

Templated response required > make it personal > customers spread the word about a company with personality

---

SUPERHERO HABITS

"What makes Superman a hero is not that
he has power, but that he has the
wisdom and maturity to use the power wisely"

- Christopher Reeve, actor

Introduction

Congratulations - you've reached the top of the ACETS pyramid - you've an amazing foundation in place and now it's time to turn your habit embedding up to the Superhero Level.

The ACETS pyramid

I've so far examined 40 different habits, each spanning a different discipline.

Back in my Customer Thermometer days, we actively embraced the old cliché of giving a customer 110%. When they wrote in with a request, we would always aim to answer it and give them more. We would always aim to anticipate what they might ask next or educate them on something aligned, which they would find useful. Customers loved it. And why wouldn't they?

I learnt such a lot during this time and want to share the more advanced concepts in this chapter, which I know can really make a difference.

If there's one over-arching theme about this layer of habits, it's this. There's too much *'vanilla'* in the helpdesk and customer service world. It's OK to stand out. It's actually preferable to stand out, to be remarkable and get talked about. One of the most overused examples of being remarkable in customer service is of course Zappos. They've developed an amazing name for themselves, because of the stories which their customers tell.

If you'd like proof – the best Zappos case study I can find is here: [Search: "*reddit zappos fell apart email*"].

So many of these well-known stories are old now, and so it's now time for *you* to create *new* stories inside *your* business. Aim to get your customers talking about you. The power to share the good and bad has never been greater. Why shouldn't your team be on the receiving end of some great PR?

It's time to become a Helpdesk Superhero.

Never assume

With verbal or ticket enquiries, first time resolution should always be the goal, where practical. You can do this by pre-empting further enquiries or making sure there's no possible way someone can question the information you've provided to them.

A great habit to get into therefore, is to "Never Assume".

Before I go further, I need to give some credit for this habit.

My Dad has taught me many things over the years. One of his most memorable pearls of wisdom is his phrase, "*never assume.*" It's now been passed down to my children. I'm often reminded of it as I go about my day.

It's important to remember that your customers are not experts on your product or your business. Whenever you talk to them or write to them, avoid lapsing into 'internal speak'.

Never assume a customer is on your wavelength.

Never assume a customer knows the intricacies of your product.

Never assume a customer is technically literate.

Just never assume.

Getting the balance right

It's a straightforward enough concept. Putting it into practice however requires finesse. If you're not careful, it's easy to offend or even come across as patronising. I've first-hand experience of doing exactly that.

If you're from the US, apologies for the next phrase:

"*I hope I'm not teaching you to suck eggs.*"

I've learnt to my cost that this very English phrase, doesn't translate well in the US. I'm English - so I can use it, with my head held high.

The phrase, translated, simply means, don't be patronising or waste people's time by explaining something that they already know or perhaps should know.

Qualify, question, anticipate and be proactive. Do that right and you'll never come across as patronising. Get in the habit of "never assuming".

How do you make a judgement call on what someone knows, when you've never met them? How do you avoid being patronising? By wording things cleverly.

Choose the right words

Even if someone *seems* as if they have a certain level of knowledge and understanding, never assume they actually do. Use that enquiry as an opportunity to check understanding and complete the picture of their knowledge.

It's a chance to educate, whether on something general and applicable to other services and companies, or on something more specific and relating to your company. Either way - if you're seen as helpful, you'll be remembered.

Once again, it's about striking the balance. If you're not certain about a requester's knowledge level, try some of these phrases:

"I'm not sure if you've used this part of the service before?"

"I'm not sure if you're familiar with the options, have you been taking a look online?"

"Would it be helpful if I took a minute to explain the options in more detail?"

"Have you had a chance to read through the brochure?"

"Can I confirm you understand all the details in the premium version?"

All of these phrases search for more information. They aren't patronising and would always be well received by a customer.

If in doubt, question some more, but never assume!

Product assumptions

Whether it's software features, utility tariffs or airline pricing, you are undoubtedly an expert in your field. Just because you are an expert, it's important to never assume any specific level of knowledge from your inbound requester.

Treat every query as an opportunity to educate. It could be that the customer knows enough to be dangerous. It's likely they will have some level of knowledge, but they probably don't know the full picture.

Acronyms

Just don't use them 😅.

Trigger > routine > reward

Complex call or response > assume the customer is expert > call completed

Complex call or response > question further and reword > educated customer

---

The next topic takes this concept a little further.

Never assume technical understanding

Consider this question to a customer:

"In order for us to diagnose the issue, we're going to need a screenshot of the error that you're seeing. Please can you send it back to me?"

Depending on the industry that you're in, there's a high percentage chance, a customer won't know how to perform that task. My Dad certainly wouldn't.

There's also a small chance a customer won't know what a screenshot is. We all know the story of someone taking a photo of their monitor and sending it on. Never assume anything!

If 50% of your audience is likely to know how to send a screenshot or perform other technical tasks, aren't you potentially wasting a requester's time by explaining how to perform this task?

Personally, I don't think so.

Remember, we're looking to get a query resolved quickly. We don't want a customer responding, with a question on how to complete a technical task or otherwise. You should therefore, always try to pre-empt this scenario.

You can do this by getting into the habit of 'never assuming'.

Being thorough

In this example, whilst a customer might be able to send a screenshot, there may be something specific you need to see and there may be a particular format you need it in. Any detail you request proactively is going to resolve the situation faster, which has to be a good thing.

How about this example response as an alternative?

"This is quite an unusual situation – and I'd like to take a look at this for you personally. To help me best advise you, I'd like to see what you're seeing on the screen.

Please can you send me a screenshot of the screen you see, immediately after you've clicked the submit button. The address bar in your browser will show "/settings/colours" at the end of the web address.

If you need some guidance on how to take a screenshot and send it back to me (don't worry – it's straightforward) – you can take a look at our simple guide, here [link to user guide].

As soon as I receive it from you – I'll come right back to you with a suggested way forward."

I don't believe this is a patronising response. It considers someone who is technically literate. It provides clarity on the deliverable that is needed, which would be helpful for someone who is technically literate. It also reassures the user that they aren't going to find this an onerous task. As a bonus, you are possibly teaching someone a new skill for the very first time and so enlightenment could be a side product of 'never assuming.'

See if you can take this concept and apply it to other situations. How might you respond to someone who needs to provide you with a trace route from a command point?

Trigger > routine > reward

Technical call or response > assume the customer is expert > call completed

Technical call or response > ensure understanding – provide proactive advice > educated, happy customer

Anticipate like a Jedi

Jedi use The Force. (And yes, that *is* the correct plural - I checked!) Helpdesk superheroes need to learn to use the equivalent, when dealing with customers.

> It's time to stop taking requests and questions at face value and to start thinking about the meaning behind them.

Anticipating what a customer *actually* wants to achieve and solving *that* problem, rather than the one they're describing to you, is quite a skill.

It's easy to rattle off an obvious response to a customer or aim to get a call finished as soon as possible to keep the relevant metrics high. In the short term, you might win. Longer term, if you're not anticipating, customers or prospects will return with more requests, to clarify, to query, and so in the end, your business will lose out, due to additional inbound requests. Spending a little extra effort on each response will avoid those repetitive customer contacts. This of course feeds into the concept of first contact resolution.

Let me first describe to you what anticipation *isn't*.

A call is completed, and a requester says thanks and goodbye, however the agent will then blindly ask,

"Is there anything else I can help you with today?"

You do already know this of course 😆.

Instead, anticipation *is* about providing pre-emptive, proactive advice or information relevant to the inbound query.

Customer: "*I can't upload this image to your site.*"

A possible agent response is: "*Unfortunately, you can only upload jpgs and gifs – pngs aren't acceptable.*"

An agent mastering their superhero habits will be thinking ahead and anticipating that a customer who has a png will typically not have the means to convert it into a jpg. Using the response above will likely mean they will either then come back to ask you if you can convert it or worse still, abandon what they're trying to achieve.

To prevent this from happening, you might try something like:

"Ah – I can see you're uploading a PNG – the system doesn't accept them I'm afraid.

Not to worry, I've converted it to a JPG for you and have uploaded it into your account – so it's ready to use!"

That's evidence of a helpdesk superhero at work.

Here's another example of anticipation:

"Thank you for placing your order with us. I hope that's resolved your query.

I've just sent you a link with the tracking information on it – so that you'll be able to track your delivery on Monday.

There's also a returns label in there, just in case it doesn't fit."

Again, this response pre-empts the type of questions a customer might ask and will save your business additional calls. More importantly, it makes you and your company look brilliant and will get customers talking about you.

I'm sure you can think of plenty of examples in your business where anticipating a customer's next question would make them extremely happy and reduce repeat inbounds.

When anticipation is constantly required, it could mean there's something wrong with a process or user interface. Always keep a record of these types of activities and feed them back to your team, so that processes can be adjusted, upstream.

A perfect example

I'm a great believer in serendipity. As I'm finishing this topic, I've received an email from a letting agent, following a query of mine earlier in the day.

I'm compelled to publish it in full below, because it's a perfect example of how to respond to a slightly nervous customer (me).

Hi Mark,

You are definitely not liable, this was the previous tenant's responsibility.

I have notified the council as well as providing a copy of the tenancy agreement. I would not advise you to pay this, this is not down to you.

I have emailed the previous tenant to obtain forwarding address details which would speed things up. Please do not worry.

Kind regards, Kimberley

Kimberley anticipated my questions and went on to reassure me as to what she's done, to ensure a successful resolution. The added touch of '*please do not* worry' is genius. It's something you rarely see written, yet those words alone put me completely at ease.

It may not surprise you to know that I love dealing with Kimberley.

Trigger > routine > reward

Customer request > answer at face value > ticket probably closed!

Customer request > anticipate and provide additional answers > ticket definitely closed!

Solve the actual problem

I've mentioned my Dad a few times – he's a model customer in many ways. He actually called me yesterday (I'm his IT helpdesk). He asked where he could learn about Excel. That was his exact question. No context, no background. Knowing him for 47 years, I knew better than to answer his question at face value.

I simply asked him, "*Why?*"

He told me he has a new volunteer role and explained he wanted to edit a form this organisation uses, as it wasn't well written.

"*Tell me about the form, Dad ...*"

"*It's a pdf – but I think it was produced in Excel.*"

We then chatted about the options and the limitations and that it could have been possibly produced using Word. I then explained the principle uses for Excel - analysis etc and that it might be easier to use Word and publish to PDF. He got it.

At the end of the call he was still interested in Excel, but for a completely different set of reasons. I then followed up with some introduction to Excel courses which he would find useful.

This simple conversation illustrates this topic brilliantly. So often, customers and prospects don't ask the right questions – and why would they? They are just looking to get something done. They're not an expert in your subject matter - you are.

Let's look at another example.

I can't remember my password

A common request, whether over the phone or via a ticket thread. A customer in this situation might just need help in resetting it so they can then carry on with their day. On the other hand, there might be more to it.

If they can't remember their password, it's possible they've not used the service in a while. They might be in danger of leaving … they might not remember how to use the service … they might not be familiar with changes or new features recently introduced. The list is endless.

This contact can now be turned into an opportunity to find out what they are actually looking to do, and guide them through it.

"You can reset your password using the reset password link on the homepage."

This is a perfectly adequate response.

However, your 'solve the actual problem' habit trigger should spring into action when this type of question is asked. You should be thinking ahead, anticipating and providing that extra 10% with your response.

"You can actually reset your password on the homepage. To help, I've sent you a password reset email – simply click the link in your email right now and choose a new password.

I can see you've not logged in for a while. You might be interested to see we've made a few changes – you can read about those here [INSERT URL]. I've also created a 10% off coupon for you to use within the next month below, which I hope you'll enjoy".

You can see the difference in approach.

You're answering the request, but also acknowledging that a forgotten password is a sign of a less than engaged customer. The response now brings them back into the fold with some additional help, an offer and shows them an agent who sounds like they know what they're doing. It's unexpected, it's surprising and it happens so rarely!

Develop this habit. Use the technique and your customers will start spreading the word about your helpdesk's superhero service.

Thinking like a Jedi

Let's look at another example.

"Do you have this widget in red?"

Whether over the phone or on a ticket, there is of course a black and white (excuse the colour related pun there) answer. Yes or No.

An acceptable response might be:

"I'm really sorry – I'm afraid this widget only comes in blue, black and white.

Thank you for contacting Widgets inc."

Superheroes think differently though. You'd recognise this request as a buying signal and would be able to respond with a much better answer.

"Yes we do, however it's out of stock at the moment.

The good news is that I can put a back order in for you right now. It'll be with us in two weeks.

If you can give me your card details, we'll get it to you as soon as you can, and you won't be charged until it's dispatched."

Or,

"No, I'm afraid we don't, however we do have it in blue – which you may not have seen on the site.

It's actually our most popular colour at the moment – we've only got 10 left in stock.

I can send you a link to the full spec, or you can give me your card details now and I'll place the order for you if that would save you some time?"

Both answers go the extra mile and combining our 'unconscious sales' habit with our new found 'superhero habits of anticipation and problem solving', these responses answer the customer's real question, which in this case was, "*I need one of your widgets to solve my problem*".

Trigger > routine > reward

Receive customer request > deal with issue at face value > you can move on

Receive customer request > use experience and questioning to understand drivers > solve the real problem

---

Teach a man to fish

In a survey in 2007 by the Customer Contact Council, over 75,000 customers were asked about their customer service interactions. It turns out the most important factor, when it comes to customer loyalty, is reducing the amount of effort a customer must expend, to solve their problem. From there, the no doubt familiar metric of Customer Effort Score was spawned and many organisations focus on that metric ahead of pure satisfaction scores.

Asking about ease of doing business with you is subtly different to asking, "*How have we done for you today?*" and will provide your business a different focus.

Whilst it's quite right to focus on this metric, it shouldn't become all-consuming. Making it easy to do business with you, doesn't mean you have to say 'yes', every time. Doing this, can make a rod for your own back and eventually your customers will rely on you for every small task.

With parenting, it's often good to say 'no', and instead, show a child how to complete something for themselves. The same applies to customers. Once again, this needs to be done the right way - taking their hand and leading them along a journey.

If a customer begins to rely on you to do everything for them, they can become a burden. Taking this approach means they will learn and grow themselves.

Putting it into practice

We all know of customers who have overreacted to a situation:

"I've just logged in and all my data is gone."

"Your service is down."

"The package hasn't arrived."

Triage is important here. You do need to check that all is well at your end and that there's not an issue affecting the entire company. If there is, then your empathy habits need to kick in. Assuming the world hasn't, in fact, come to an end, it's now your job to guide a customer through the issue they're perceiving.

> Imagine for a moment, you're Yoda.
> Teach your customers to use The Force.

Rather than dropping everything and heading down a tunnel of potentially time-wasting diagnosis, take a pause and put the onus back on the customer, temporarily.

"Could you tell me a little more about what's happening here? Have any of your colleagues noticed any issues?"

"Could you send me a screenshot of what you're seeing or send the error code? I can then take a look at this for you."

This is getting the customer to do some work for themselves... maybe their Internet connection is down? Maybe they're using the wrong login? It's OK to ask a customer to perform some self-diagnosis.

Asking these questions helps them to think rationally about a situation and gets them into the mindset of fixing issues for themselves.

Bear in mind that if your helpdesk was closed, they'd perhaps do this self-diagnosis for themselves, when no one else was around to help. All this habit is doing, is asking them to think a little for themselves. They will learn more about your service in the process.

You can go too far here. Be aware of when the time is right to jump in and get involved. Always make sure they know you're there for them if they need it.

Trigger > routine > reward

Customer demand > drop everything to respond > customer will feel fulfilled

Customer demand > help them to help themselves > customer feels empowered and will become less of a burden over time

Managing 'quexpectations'

Customers desperately want to feel communicated with. They want to be kept uptodate, with proactive communication and for timelines to be adhered to. They also want to feel like they're dealing with real human beings who are empowered to get things done.

With any helpdesk operating at scale, a ticketing application will be used to manage inbound tickets and replies. More often than not, if a customer raises a ticket, they will receive an automated response, acknowledging their query. This is a good thing – it's a confirmation and gives the customer some reassurance that their issue is going to be dealt with.

Managing queue expectations is such a simple superhero habit to embrace, yet so few helpdesk agents or managers will exploit this automation. It's time to change that and set the tone across your helpdesk ethos.

Here's what's considered a 'normal' email auto response when a requester raises a ticket:

- Please type your reply above this line -

Thank you for contacting Support. Your request (#2128552) has been received and is being reviewed by our support staff.

The Widget support team.

I sometimes wonder whether customer service staff even know that these messages are customisable. They always will be, irrespective of the helpdesk system used. Yes, there needs to be process and systems in place, however they need to be in place *for the benefit of the helpdesk*. The customer just wants their query answered as efficiently as possible.

Here's an alternative approach, using the same ticket template:

Dear Mark,

We wanted you to know that we've received your email.

We are looking into your query right now and always aim to be back to you within a couple of hours. Quite often it's faster, because we know you want to get on with your day.

Magically, we've given your request a reference number (#2128552). Feel free to use that if you'd rather speak to us on (0800 123123).

Also, don't forget we've FAQ at widgets.com/faq too.

Bear with us – we're the best in the business and we'll be back to you shortly.

Best wishes,

Harry, Support team lead
PS Happy Monday.

Put your customer shoes on for a moment. Imagine receiving an auto response like this example, to a ticket you'd raised. You'd smile, wouldn't you? You'd be delighted that you were dealing with a competent company who knew what they were doing because of the confidence they'd instilled in you through some very simple words.

In most situations, customers are happy enough to wait for a helpful, accurate response, providing they have been communicated with during the process of waiting.

In the example response template above, I've set an expectation of 2 hours. Imagine as a customer how you might feel if you received a response within 30 mins? Delighted? a raving fan and something to tell others how good your service is? Definitely.

You can of course amend these numbers to suit your business. Changing the template to 24 hours, to give yourself some slack and then responding in 4 hours will still delight a customer. It's all about meeting or beating expectations.

Here's a challenge for you:

Change your ticket autoresponder today, to a message to make a human smile.

Trigger > routine > reward

Customer response needed > use the default > anything for an easy life

Customer response needed > make it the best you can > your company has a personality

---

Refer, refer, refer

Your actions on a helpdesk aren't always about cementing relationships in the future. They can also affect the here and now.

One of the most powerful methods of winning new business is the 'referral'. If you're lucky, referrals can happen without you even knowing.

> *"84% of B2B decision makers start the buying process with a referral."*
>
> Heinz Marketing, Redmond, WA

Asking for referrals is an underused technique in a sales process and is a great habit to get into. Remember that people who have had a great experience with you, particularly if you've helped them through an issue, are indebted to you at that point. The law of reciprocity kicks in. People are looking for a way to pay back. Asking for a referral at this point in a conversation is ideal timing.

This type of approach of course needs to be agreed at a team or company level. If your business is not already actively asking for referrals, it is something worth raising. Once you've done it successfully a couple of times, it becomes addictive.

"Just before you go, is there anyone you could recommend us to? I can send you a link, to send onto them if that'd be helpful?"

It can get more sophisticated too...

"For anyone who does sign up from your referral, we'll credit your account with $25."

The financial incentive is often not needed. Most people are just happy to informally recommend a company they've had a good experience with. Your task is to prompt them to do it and to make the process pain free. Providing a paragraph of text or a link to forward on, also works well.

> *"Offering a reward increases referral likelihood, but the size of the reward does not matter."*
>
> American Marketing Association

Whilst I'm sure that's true, don't expect someone to go too far out of their way for you. You must make it easy.

If you're ever unsure about this concept, I'd ask you remember this:

> *"If you don't ask, you don't get."*
>
> My Dad

That's the final dose of inspiration from my Dad. (He'll be asking for commission at this rate). He's right. What's the worst that could happen by asking that question? A customer that might say 'no'. You won't offend them, providing you ask in the right way. The upside is that more people get to hear about your company and they may end up becoming a customer.

If you don't have a referral programme on your helpdesk, put some time aside to get one in place as a matter of urgency. You and your team are on the frontline of your organisation and so there's no one better placed to be proactive with customers within your day to day interactions.

> **Trigger > routine > reward**
>
> *Happy customer >* "Thanks for the call" *> Call dealt with*
>
> **Happy customer >** "Referral offer" **> new business potential**

Get personal

Whether over the phone or over email, you can make a customer smile and remember you, by personalising your responses. Human customer service has been a theme woven throughout the book and when you start to get personal with customers (in the right way), you will quickly see the benefits.

This is a great habit to cultivate, because customers have come to expect impersonal, robotic responses from helpdesks and so your opportunity to shine is open ended.

The impersonal nature of the helpdesk world staggers me, because I don't believe there is a law in business, which dictates you mustn't have a personality or make people smile. I'm not advocating telling jokes, however I'm absolutely advocating getting into the habit of treating your customers like they're humans, with emotions, who like to interact with personalities.

Use names

If you're on the phone to a customer, try interjecting the caller's name into the conversation. Imagine someone listening in to your conversation – aim to make the observer think you'd known the client for years:

"I'm going to get right on that, Suzanne."

"Suzanne, have you already reported this issue?"

"Give me a moment, Suzanne – I'm just looking up the information now."

It's powerful to continually use a caller's name. The alternative is so less personal, less sincere and so much more formal:

"I'm going to get right on that, Madam / Sir ..."

Using this personal approach, does two things – it's a reminder you're having a conversation with a *real person* – a customer who has a job and a life and a legitimate reason behind his or her frustration, rather than a faceless 'sir' or 'madam'. Secondly, assuming you can get the tone right, it will make the *customer* feel like they're truly valued and you really care.

Whilst on the subject of names – if you don't already, make sure you use your name. Introduce yourself when appropriate – and ideally, not in a scripted way at the start of a call, if that's within your power.

Remembering

In smaller businesses, you will get to recognise and eventually know your customers over time. Relationships will naturally form. It's important to acknowledge this and not to shy away from striking up these relationships.

> Pretending not to notice the same person is raising tickets on a regular basis would eventually come across as rude and uncaring.

The opposite applies. Embrace the fact a customer has regular contact with you or your team. Make the most of it – treat them warmly and it will be rewarding for both sides.

Customer Thermometer has many large corporate customers. During my time there, we remembered their birthdays, we sent them gift packs, we asked about their children and we were concerned about their welfare. As a result, we were remembered. These simple acts created tremendous loyalty and got us talked about and referred regularly.

You should develop the habit too, whether as an individual, or as a team. Make a point of adding a:

"PS, I hope Phil is still enjoying his travels."

at the end of a ticket reply (or through conversation).

Use your empathy skills to know when you should be more business-focused and to the point. 'Feel' the right thing to do and always sense the tone, before adding that personal touch – it's not always wanted.

Across your team, use CRM technology to make an internal note about an important customer's birthday or major event. Share experiences, talk about those important customer relationships and make it a team ethos to exploit the personal touch.

Canned responses

I've talked about the essential use of knowledgebases and not reinventing the wheel, throughout this habits journey. Canned responses, within a ticketing system, are another important component of this process, to shorten reply times and to ensure the most accurate and uptodate information is sent on to customers.

There is a danger however that a canned response, *looks like a canned response*. For the avoidance of doubt, that's not a good thing.

Canned responses are a real time saver, but can be impersonal

Your canned response database is an essential tool, however like all tools, it's about how you use it, which will make or break it. Whenever you add a canned response, always read it through. Make sure that it's 100% relevant and doesn't contain information which isn't needed in that response.

For longer canned paragraphs, do what you can to personalise them. Either edit the canned text or ensure that the paragraphs before and after have some form of personal touch.

I've seen responses which are simply cut and paste from a knowledgebase, with little attempt at a greeting or a sign off. I find that insulting – it gives me an impression of your company I know you wouldn't want me to have.

I deliberately didn't make a purchase from a software company last month, because of the poor, clearly canned, response I received to a presales question. Whilst the software fitted what I needed, the complete lack of care over a simple response, gave me a bad feeling.

It takes seconds to make it right. Get into the habit of taking the time.

Trigger > routine > reward

Templated response required > no personalisation > easy life

Templated response required > make it personal > customers spread the word about a company with personality

Painting pictures

As we reach the penultimate topic in this plethora of customer service habits, this is one of my absolute favourites. It's a favourite because the technique is tried and tested (by me and my team) over the last 8 years and I've rarely, if ever, seen another company use it, particularly the advanced technique I outline below.

If you embrace the concept, yet again, it means you've a chance to shine. You've a chance to stand out from the crowd and to be remarkable – the whole point of this book. I want your helpdesk to become a 'feature' of your business, not an overhead.

Simplify with screenshots

For years, I was asked for technical explanations, to explain which feature to use and what setting to add where, within our app. I'd often start writing a reply with a detailed description and then pause.

> I quickly reminded myself that
> a picture paints a thousand words,
> deleted my text and reached for my screenshot tool.

I'd snip the relevant screen, annotate it and then write a much simpler and therefore clearer response back to the customer. They were always delighted. The visual cue makes things so much easier to understand, particularly for someone who isn't technically literate.

The same technique (and habit) can be used outside of the technical domain. Clarifying how to buy on your website, explaining where a particular piece of information can be found or even screenshotting an application such as PowerPoint to explain how to get something done can all be massive time savers.

The key to success with this habit is to make sure the screenshot is both accurate and well annotated. Recently, I was sent a screenshot of an example invoice generated for a software tool I was evaluating. The screenshot showed a VAT line, however, it showed zero, implying it hadn't been generated correctly. This meant a further round of replies until I got to the right answer. There's a final helpdesk team who will be getting a copy of this book 😜 .

Annotating is important too. Sending someone a 1920 x 1080px screen shot, containing a complex screen of information, without arrows, circles or words of explanation is the opposite of helpful. Any decent screenshot tool will allow you to annotate and paste straight into the ticket.

Annotated screenshots get the message across succinctly

If you've an older ticketing system, allowing plain text only (I can only apologise), then you will need to upload the image to a suitable server and link to it. Tickets allowing rich text and images will allow you to paste your screenshot inline, within the response. Attachments are less helpful, as they aren't within the flow of the narrative.

Screenshot tool recommendations

Software changes all the time, and so this list may be out of date now, particularly if you're reading this in 2050. That said, here's some recommendations of great tools you could add to your workflow:

Screenpresso - Windows app (free and premium)

Lightshot - Mac & Windows app (free)

Awesome screenshot - Chrome Extension (free)

Gadwin Print Screen - Windows app (free and premium)

Marker.io - Chrome Extension (free and premium)

There are dozens more available. If in doubt, a quick search will find the right tool for your team.

Revolutionise with video

So, if you want to feel like a true helpdesk superhero, then the next step is to help customers via the power of video. Personalise your responses where appropriate to explain specific workflows or concepts, by using a screencam tool and ideally, voiceover to deliver a really powerful message.

That may sound daunting, but once it becomes a habit and part of your workflow, you won't look back.

I have used screencam software for many years to send customers proposals, ideas and to respond to tickets. Without fail, it wows people. The fact that I'd taken the trouble to explain my message or answer a question with a bespoke video (which might have taken me all of 10 minutes to produce) was seen as revolutionary. Videos can of course be easily shared - so if your customer needs to help a colleague or get buy in for your service - they can pass on the full story via your video.

> 'Practice makes progress', as my children tell me.

Put your toe in the water and try it. Get used to adding your voice over and explaining your message to a customer. The best time to try this out is with presales. If someone wants to know whether your service can perform a specific task – show it to them! Make it personal – go the extra mile. That in itself will help to sell the service.

Video tool recommendations

Again, this list will no doubt be out of date quickly, however there are some well established online tools which will be around for many years. Desktop apps such as Camtasia are a little more specialist and expensive, so I'd recommending starting with the services I list below:

ShareX – Windows app (free)

Screencastify – Chrome extension (free)

Loom – Chrome extension (free)

Screenpresso – Windows app (free and premium)

Kap – MacOS (free)

A final word

Using these tools adds complexity to ticket responses *if you're not careful*. My message to you is simple. Don't allow them to add complexity! Choose a tool that's right for your team and then add it to your workflow.

Spend a team meeting learning how to use the concept to its full potential and then share knowledge on what works. If it creates barriers to responding to tickets, then you've got the process wrong. Using tools and techniques like this should benefit both you and your customer. Keep practicing until you get it right.

Link this workflow with your knowledgebase updates. If you don't have simple gifs or videos explaining where to move a mouse or what text to input or how to set up a configuration within your knowledgebase, then you're missing a trick. If in doubt, refer back to the "Link externally" topic.

Using this technique on an individual customer basis, means that you can show them how to use *their* account, with *their* data. It brings the explanation alive and makes it real, as opposed to using a generic explainer. This is perfect in the presales environment.

As ever, be very mindful of privacy considerations and ensure any hosted videos expire regularly and are hosted securely.

Trigger > routine > reward

Difficult explanation required > write more words > detailed response sent

Difficult explanation required > switch to the 'picture' workflow > customer 'gets it' faster

Roll your own

You've now read all 49 Helpdesk Habits.

Most will be applicable to you and your business. A few may not – due to the nature of your role and whether you're on the phone, chat or email.

I hope the majority have started to make an impact on you and your and team. I also hope you've had a chance to talk them through and have begun to embed them into your day.

Working on one at a time is smart. Over time, they'll compound.

Helpdesk Habit #50 is left 'blank' for you to fill in. When you put this book down, I want this to be the start of your habit journey, not the end. I've given you plenty of ideas for improvement and change, however I'm not expert on *your* helpdesk environment. You are.

What habit can you come up with, either alone or with colleagues, which you feel needs creating? What bad behaviour needs addressing? What needs improving? What needs cultivating?

Pick just one idea and replace the title above with the new one. Fill in the box below too:

Trigger > routine > reward

Helpdesk Habits is available as an online video program and certification.

Register for a free trial at **helpdeskhabits.com**

If you're looking for a dynamic way of embedding these habits with your team, the author, Mark Copeman presents them, in the form of a comprehensive video course with resources and desktop wallpapers.

Mark's team produce customised versions for larger organisations.

As a thank you for buying and reading this book, use the coupon code: **HHBOOK** for 10% off solo and team memberships.

Helpdesk Habits event speaking

Mark Copeman speaks regularly around the world on the subjects of human customer service, change and habit creation.

Find out more at helpdeskhabits.com/speaking